Theology and Ecology in Dialogue
in Dialogue
The Wisdom of *Laudato Si'*

Dermot A. Lane
Foreword by Seán McDonagh SCC

'Postscript' and 'St Kevin and the Blackbird', from *The Spirit Level*,
by Seamus Heaney, reprinted with permission of Faber and Faber Ltd.
Every effort has been made to trace and contact the copyright holder of 'Gifting'
by Catherine De Vinck. Please contact Messenger Publications with any enquiries
or information regarding the copyright holder.

ISBN 978 1 78812 194 1

Designed by Messenger Publications Design Department
Typeset in Adobe Caslon Pro & Bernhard Modern
Printed by Johnswood Press Ltd, Ireland

Messenger Publications,
37 Leeson Place, Dublin D02 E5V0
www.messenger.ie

CONTENTS

Acknowledgements

THIS BOOK has been in the making for some time. It was stimulated in particular by various events in the last five years: the publication by Pope Francis of *Laudato Si': On Care for our Common Home*, May 2015; the UN Paris Agreement on Climate in December 2015, signed by 198 nations, and the ever-increasing number of reports on the gravity of climate change and the loss of biodiversity.

Research for this book was made possible by different people whom I wish to thank publicly. Diarmuid Martin, Archbishop of Dublin, supported the idea of a sabbatical in 2017, and Eamon Walsh, Auxiliary Bishop of Dublin and Head of the Office for Clergy, paved the way for the sabbatical to happen in 2018. My sabbatical leave took place in the welcoming Jesuit School of Theology in Berkeley, California, from September 2018 to January 2019.

I wish to thank Messenger Publications who, in the person of Donal Neary SJ, welcomed the manuscript at a time of uncertainty. It has been a pleasure working with Donal, Cecilia West and their very professional staff. Donal and his team enabled the book to be published in May 2020 to coincide with the fifth anniversary of the publication of *Laudato Si'*.

A particular word of thanks to my secretary Hazel Rooke, who typed and retyped different versions of the book over the last number of years with great patience. Hazel is not just a secretary. In truth she ironed out textual wrinkles and asked valuable questions about the content along the way.

A special debt of gratitude is due to long-time friend and colleague, Terrence W. Tilley, Professor Emeritus of Theology, Fordham University, New York. Terry read and reread the entire manuscript at short notice. He offered insightful suggestions and nuanced corrections along the way. Whatever mistakes remain are, of course, entirely mine.

Lastly, I wish to thank the people of Balally Parish, where I have ministered as parish priest for twenty-five years and now serve as parish chaplain. Over the years parishioners would have heard variations of the book in different disguises and they often offered constructive feedback. To all of the above people, and others in the background, I offer my thanks for much support and encouragement.

FOREWORD

IT IS important to have a clear understanding of the scale of change in the theology of creation which Dermot Lane presents in his very welcome book. The historical background to this change goes back to the Council of Trent (1545–1563) after which the Roman missal was published by Pope Paul V in 1570. In that Missal, the post-communion prayer for the Sundays of Advent reads as follows: *Domine, doce nos terrena despicere, et amare celestia.* (Lord, teach us to despise the things of earth and to love the things of heaven). This prayer with its dualistic and escapist theology had little appreciation for the intrinsic value of the natural world. Every year for almost 400 years this text was read each Advent in the Catholic Church. This lack of concern for creation was also present in many popular prayers throughout the entire second millennium.

In this new book, Lane does not merely tweak this teaching, or attempt to present it in a more nuanced way. On the contrary, he challenges and refutes it based on the teachings of scripture and the findings of modern science. In line with his theological anthropology, humans are related to everything existing in our universe at present, and are connected with everything that has existed going back to the birth of the universe 13.8 billion years ago.

In line with the evolutionary dynamism and the writings of Karl Rahner and Pierre Teilhard de Chardin, Lane believes that the whole of creation is gifted with self-transcendent possibilities through the enduring action of the Holy Spirit. He argues that 'if we took the spirit seriously, we would have a different theology of the Church and creation today.' This theology 'from below' involves two elements. First we must grasp the extensive understanding of the idea of *ruach* (spirit) in Jewish theology and, secondly, we must explore the primordial experiences of the spirit, not just in history, but, also in the encounter and experience of the spirit in nature, not only in the past but also in the present.

Lane is not content with articulating a new deep pneumatology; he claims that such a pneumatology should go hand-in-hand with a new Christology, one that is intimately linked to the natural word. Like every one of us, Christ is a child of the universe. Most significantly the spirit in Judaism is an earth-loving spirit dwelling in the dust, nostrils and the matter of creation. The theology of the Word is also crucial; as it sees the cosmic activity of the Word descending down into human history when the Word became flesh and lived among us. This cosmic Christology confers a new dignity on creation, recovers the intrinsic value of the earth's processes and systems and points to an underlying solidarity between the earth community and the human community. *Laudato Si'* affirms that if all things are destined to be part of a new creation in Christ, then other creatures must be respected for their value in themselves and not just for utilitarian reasons.

Furthermore, Lane develops an eschatology which moves beyond our concern for the last things – death, judgment, heaven and hell. He is unhappy with the way this watered down eschatology has left a hole in the rest of theology, leaving us bereft of 'essential elements such as the subversive and prophetic role of hope, the centrality of the resurrection to Christian faith and the link between creation and eschatology.'

It is worth pointing out that our Western culture and our Christian faith has very little respect for the oceans. Though seventy per cent of the planet's surface is covered by the sea, we know more about the surface of Mars and the Moon than we know about the oceans. Without the oceans our planet would be as inhospitable as Mars: no meadows, no forests, no birds, no animals and no humans. Life began in the oceans 3.8 billion years ago. It evolved and was nurtured there for more than 3 billion years before it began to move onto the land. Every diocese in Ireland touches the oceans, yet I do not know a single one that has drawn up a reflection on the presence of God in the oceans, chronicled the damage humans have done to date and devised a concrete plan to protect the oceans in the future. If Christian communities could become engaged in this kind of action, Lane believes that 'eschatology [could] inspire and motivate ecology practices that will enhance the well-being of our common home.' He also claims that eschatology can begin to bridge the gap between human beings and non-human creatures, between the human community and the earth community, between creation and society. This new focus is 'intended to widen the scope of the resurrection from being exclusively anthropocentric to being cosmo-centred.'

Lane deals with the conflicts that surround the classic text from Genesis 1:26–23, which speaks of 'tilling the earth and subduing it and having dominion of the fish.' He makes the point that the text is ambiguous and is coloured by the belief in modern times that humans are licensed by the Bible to exploit the earth's eco-systems. Even the Fathers at the Second Vatican Council subscribed to 'domination theology.' *Gaudium et Spes* (*The Pastoral Constitution on Church in the Modern World*), states that the world is there for the exclusive use of humankind: 'man created in God's image received a mandate to subject to himself all that it contains and govern the world with justice and holiness' (*Gaudium et Spes*, 34).

Worship is central to the Christian experience and to Lane's book. He quotes the saying from the Fathers that '*Lex Orandi, Lex Credendi*' (we pray as we believe). Unfortunately, there is not much reference to creation in the liturgy of the Eucharist, which means that our liturgical prayers are almost schizophrenic. We believe one thing, and at the same time celebrate something quite different and often at odds with what we believe. This is tragic, since thanking God for the blessing of creation was present in the Eucharist prayers from the very beginning. In the Eucharist prayer found in the *Apostolic Tradition,* which dates from 215 CE, God is thanked for the gift of creation. This thanksgiving appears in the second paragraph, immediately after a thanksgiving to the Father for sending Jesus as Saviour and Redeemer.[1]

If the Eucharist challenges us to share the earth not only with our fellow human beings but also with other species in the earth community, then we would have to admit that we have responded to the challenge poorly. Every eco-system on our planet has been exploited by humans for their benefit only. We have very little concern for the well-being of the millions of species who share this planet with us and, of course, we have given them no basic rights.

In his discussion of the liturgy Lane criticises the sexist language used in the Eucharist prayers 'for which there is no excuse.' The same is true of the liturgy of the hours. In Morning Prayer for Thursday of the First Week Psalm 56 says that 'my soul lies down among the lions, who would destroy the sons of men.' In the same way, the *Benedictus* states that 'so his love for our fathers is fulfilled.' Not a word about mothers! How could anyone encourage young women to pray these texts? The tragedy is, I believe, that neither the leaders in the Church, in Rome or bishops in local English-speaking dioceses are aware that the sexist language used in Church worship is alienating many people, especially young women, from experiencing the Gospel.

This new book about ecology and theology is not just about a special area of theology that might be of interest to scholars. Rather Lane argues persuasively that ecological questions should permeate the whole of theology and the practice of Christian faith. This book deals with *the* most important issue of our time both for the world and the Church, for non-believers and believers alike. As we have seen, until *Laudato Si'*, the Catholic Church was meagre and patchy in responding to the destruction of our natural world. So, it is wonderful to see a competent theologian, in dialogue with other theologians, investigating both our biblical sources and modern science to fashion a new vision of our Christian faith that takes the 'sign of the times' most seriously.

Theology and Ecology in Dialogue also outlines a new way of being in the world where Christians begin to listen to the cry of the poor and the earth, and therefore respond with a new, transformative Christian praxis. And finally, this book points in the direction of a new liturgy, where all join together in praising God for the wonders of creation and thereby become converted to a new way of living and acting and feeling in the natural world. If we fail in this vital task, in the words of Pope Francis, the earth will become more and more like an immense pile of filth for the next generation.

Seán McDonagh SCC

CHAPTER 1

Theology and Ecology

THE PURPOSE of this opening chapter is to map out the context for what is to follow. The subject of 'ecology and theology' is vast and therefore requires not only context but some parameters. To that end a brief and selective overview of *Laudato Si'* (*LS*) will set the stage. The chapters that follow are selective in the areas they cover and do not claim or pretend in any way to be a comprehensive overview of ecology and theology, or of *Laudato Si'*.

Introduction to *Laudato Si'*

This chapter will focus on the adoption of an integral ecology and what this means for the important dialogue that can and should take place between ecology and theology. In opening up this dialogue between ecology and theology, the question arises: is theology up to this new challenge? Can theology see the ecological crisis as not only a challenge but also an opportunity for the renewal of theology in itself, and an opportunity for theology to participate in public debate about the environment? Within a few years of the publication of *Laudato Si'*, Pope Francis challenged theology to renew itself in the service of the Gospel and the care of creation.

   2015 is an important date for anyone interested in the environmental crisis and the ever-increasing loss of biodiversity. On 24 May 2015, Pope Francis wrote an encyclical entitled: *Laudato Si': On Care for our*

Common Home. It was addressed to 'every person living on the planet' and expressed a deep desire 'to enter into dialogue with all people about our common home'.[1] The encyclical was received positively by scientists and politicians, and hailed by believers and non-believers alike as a significant document. *An Islamic Declaration on Climate*, released in August 2015 in Istanbul, spoke positively of *Laudato Si'*. In the summer of 2015 a statement by US Jewish rabbis warmly welcomed the encyclical.

In December 2015 a United Nations conference on climate, COP21, was held in Paris. It hailed the encyclical as an important contribution to a worldwide problem. In fact, Pope Francis had published his encyclical deliberately in anticipation of the upcoming conference. The conference, with the participation of 198 delegates, acknowledged openly the value of *Laudato Si'*. According to respected journalist Austin Ivereigh, many international figures associated with the climate debate, such as Al Gore, Lord Nicholas Stern (the World Bank economist) and Jeffrey Sachs spoke openly of the influence of *Laudato Si'* on the proceedings of the Paris Agreement. According to one commentator, 'the common wisdom is that, without *Laudato Si'*, it is far from sure that the Paris Agreement would have been signed'.[2]

Laudato Si' has been praised globally and enthusiastically received and described in the following way:

- A prophetic challenge for the twenty-first century[3]
- A game-changer[4]
- The most important encyclical in the life of the Catholic Church[5]
- A wake-up call for the world and the Church[6]
- A moral milestone[7]
- A pastoral landmark
- A revolutionary document[8]

My own view is that *Laudato Si'* is a theological treasure chest waiting to be explored.

It is important to note that *Laudato Si'* has a background in the teaching of Francis's predecessors. John Paul II issued a document for the World Day of Peace in 1990, entitled 'Peace with God the Creator, Peace with all creation'. Benedict XVI wrote a similar document, entitled 'If you want to cultivate peace, protect creation' (2010). In addition, Benedict addressed the question of ecology and theology in his encyclical *Caritas in Veritate* (7 July 2009), in which he spoke about the 'grammar' of the natural world. Francis builds on the work of his predecessors and goes well beyond it by connecting ecology with theology, politics, the modern sciences, liturgy and morality.

Laudato Si' is made up of six chapters. The opening chapter offers an analysis of 'What is Happening to Our Common Home?' This is followed by 'The Gospel of Creation'. Chapter 3 examines 'The Human Roots of the Ecological Crisis', which offers, among other things, a nuanced critique of the technocratic paradigm without ignoring what can be of value in modern technology. Chapter 4 addresses the meaning of integral ecology. The next chapter maps out 'Lines of Approach and Action'. The final chapter highlights the importance of 'Ecological Education and Spirituality'.

A number of radical calls are scattered throughout the encyclical. These include:

- The call for a 'bold cultural revolution' (*LS*, 114)
- An 'intense dialogue' between religion and science (*LS*, 62)
- The adoption of an 'integral ecology' (*LS*, Chapter 4)
- An ecological education and spirituality (*LS*, Chapter 6)
- A radical ecological conversion (*LS*, 5, 216, 217, 219)
- A call to hear the cry of the poor and the earth (*LS*, 49)

The encyclical also raises huge deeply connected moral questions, such as the need to critique market-driven capitalism; the importance of recognising that climate change affects the poor most; an emphasis on solidarity between the developing world and the so-called developed world, between the generations and between humans and the natural world; the centrality of justice: social justice, climate justice and intergenerational justice.

These ethical questions have rightly been to the fore in most debates about the environment, and should continue to be central. However, the time has now come to take an explicitly theological approach to the challenges and opportunities that the climate emergency raises. It would be contrary to the spirit, philosophy and theology of *Laudato Si'* to separate theology and ethics. Instead, a theological approach should be seen as complementary to ethics. Further, by focusing on ecology and theology, it is hoped to show that ecology is not an add-on to theology; instead, ecology should permeate the whole of theology, moral, systematic and liturgical.

Integral Ecology

A little historical background will help us to grasp the far-reaching significance of the turn to integral ecology in *Laudato Si'*. In 1866 Ernest Haeckel, a German biologist, coined the term *oecologie* from the Greek *oikos*, meaning household/dwelling place. One of the earliest definitions of ecology goes back to Haeckel, who described it as 'the study of relationships between organisms and their environment, both organic and inorganic'. Along with others, Haeckel drew attention to the importance of Charles Darwin and the need to take account of the complex relations that act as the conditions of the struggle for existence. Darwin is described by most environmental historians as a key figure in the history of ecology over the last couple of centuries.

Another important figure in the history of ecological thinking is Eugene Odum who, in 1970, described ecology as an 'integrated discipline' committed to holism and opposed to materialistic reductions of reality. As an integrated discipline, ecology seeks to bring together the natural and the social sciences, the integration of economic and environmental values, and the interface of science and society. For some reason, Odum's integrated ecology neglected the humanities, philosophy and religious studies.

In 1977 Arne Næss came up with the concept of 'deep ecology', which claimed that non-human organisms and their environments have intrinsic value and are not just of value as objects for humans to use. The idea of 'deep ecology' has become important in contemporary spirituality and in Christology.[9] The term 'integral ecology' surfaced first in a marine ecology textbook by Hilary Moore in 1958. Moore saw ecology as a discipline that crosses the boundaries of divergent fields of study. In effect, integral ecology is about the realisation that environmental issues cannot be dissociated from social, political, economic and cultural issues.

In the mid-1990s, the language of integral ecology appeared in the theologies of Thomas Berry, who emphasised cosmology, in Leonardo Boff, who wrote about the cry of the earth and of the poor, and in Ken Wilbur, who had a keen awareness of the unity of all life in the universe. In 2000 Wilbur came up with a well-known quadrant describing the different levels of relationship within ecology: subjective ('I'); inter-subjective ('We'); objective ('It'); and inter-objective ('Its').

Within these voices and many others, integral ecology seeks to overcome modern dualisms of:

- Sacred and secular
- Objective and subjective
- Spirit and matter
- Anthropocentrism and biocentrism
- Political and mystical
- Spiritual and material
- Nature and culture

Among inter-faith voices, there emerged a focus on human dignity, solidarity, the common good and the mystical.

One commentator on integral ecology, Guattari, sums up the challenge facing integral ecology in the following way:

> How do we change mentalities, how do we re-invent social practices that would give back to humanity – if it ever had it – a sense of responsibility for its own survival, but equally for the future of all life on the planet, for animals and vegetable species, likewise for incorporeal species such as music, arts, cinema, relations with time, love and compassion for others, the feeling of fusion at the heart of the cosmos.[10]

Sean Kelly, philosopher at the Californian Institute of Integral Studies, examines the diversity of ecological visions and, in the light of that diversity, outlines what he calls 'Five Principles of Integral Ecology'. For Kelly, ecology is integral:

- If it is situated in an evolutionary context
- If it is planetary in scope
- If it reaches beyond disciplinary boundaries
- If it affirms a sacred or enchanted universe and
- If it is committed to practical engagements[11]

Kelly goes beyond what he calls 'the spiritually deadening, mechanistic and materialistic views of reality that much of contemporary culture takes for granted'. The time has come to let go 'of the perspective of mainstream science' which sees the cosmos as 'composed of essentially lifeless particles, which, without inherent meaning or purpose, have more or less accidentally given rise to life and self-conscious beings such as ourselves'.[12]

A good example of these perspectives on integral ecology can be found in the *Earth Charter* (2000), an international declaration drawn up after six years of worldwide consultation. The document recognises that ecology, economics, and social, cultural, ethical and spiritual issues are all closely connected. Chapter 2 deals explicitly with 'ecological integrity', which commits the international community to the protection and restoration of the earth's ecological system, with special concern for biological diversity and the natural processes that sustain life.

It is against the background of this selective history of ecology, the entry of ecology into public discourse, and the *Earth Charter* that we can now situate the ground-breaking encyclical *Laudato Si': On Care for Our Common Home*. Integral ecology is a red thread running through *Laudato Si'* and, in addition, it also has a chapter to itself, entitled 'Integral Ecology' (Chapter 4:137–142).

Integral ecology is mentioned explicitly at least ten times in the encyclical. St Francis of Assisi is held up as an 'example par excellence … of an integral ecology lived out joyfully and authentically' and, as such, 'is patron saint of all who study and work in the area of ecology'. He also 'shows us just how inseparable the bond is between concern for nature, justice for the poor, commitment to society, and interior peace' (*LS*, 10). Further, St Francis helps us to see that integral ecology 'calls for openness to categories which transcend the language of mathematics and biology, and takes us to the heart of what it is to be human' (*LS*,

11). *Laudato Si'* acknowledges that some will deny 'the rich contribution which religions can make towards an integral ecology' (*LS*, 62), and this helps us to understand why the encyclical is a blend of human principles and Christian perspectives. In addition, 'integral ecology needs to take account of the value of labour', as noted by John Paul II in *Laborem Exercens* (*LS*, 124).

The encyclical opens Chapter 4, 'Integral Ecology', by noting that 'since everything is connected' this chapter will 'consider some elements of an integral ecology' (*LS*, 137). In this chapter it is recognised that integral ecology:

- is inseparable from the notion of the common good; (*LS*, 159)
- holds that 'we can no longer speak of sustainable development apart from inter-generational solidarity'; (*LS*, 159)
- requires a recognition of the vision that the 'environment is part of a logic of receptivity' and, therefore, 'is on loan to each generation which must hand it on to the next' (*LS*, 159), and so integral ecology
- embraces the importance of 'inter-generational solidarity'; (*LS*, 159)
- 'includes taking time to recover a serene harmony with creation, reflecting on our lifestyle and our ideals, and contemplating the Creator who lives among us … whose presence must not be contrived but found, uncovered'; (*LS*, 225)
- 'is made up of simple gestures which break with the logic of violence, exploitation and selfishness. In the end, a world of exacerbated consumption is at the same time a world which mistreats life in all its forms'. (*LS*, 230)

Another way of describing an integral ecology, which the encyclical takes up, is the need within ecology for 'inter-disciplinary research' (*LS*, 135), 'free from all economic or political pressure' (*LS*, 183), and 'capable of a new, integral and inter-disciplinary approach to handling different aspects of the crisis' (*LS*, 197).

In this context of solidarity, the encyclical asks: 'What kind of world do we want to leave to those who come after us?' and goes on then to respond to its own question: 'We may well be leaving to the coming generations debris, desolation, and filth' (*LS*, 161).

These perspectives on integral ecology come together in a powerful and radical way when the encyclical points out:

> We are faced not with two separate crises, one environmental and the other social, but rather one complex crisis which is both social and environmental. *(LS*, 139)

The link between the ecological and the social is inseparable. To resolve this 'complex crisis' will require 'strategies' that 'demand an integrated approach to combatting poverty, restoring dignity to the excluded and, at the same time, protect nature' (*LS*, 139). This means realising that 'a true ecological approach must integrate questions of justice in debates on the environment so as to hear the cry of the earth and the poor' (*LS*, 49). These dimensions of integral ecology in *Laudato Si'* require a move beyond the disciplinary boundaries of the science of ecology. This means that ecology cannot be separated from social or cultural or economic or ethical or religious issues, or from the hard sciences and the soft sciences. This is indeed a radical programme, reaching deep down into the underlying causes of the ecological crisis, such as market-driven capitalism, anthropocentrism, enlightenment rationality, the dualisms of modernity, the new technologies and consumerism, and the mechanisation of nature. The devastation of the Amazon river basin is a good example of a vicious problem needing a multi-faceted solution as proposed by *Laudato Si'*. Consistent with this radical thinking on integral ecology in *Laudato Si'* was the Synod of Bishops in Rome on 'The Amazon: New Paths for the Church and for an Integral Ecology', which, in turn, was followed up by the post-synodal apostolic exhortation *Querida Amazonia* (February 2020).

Another example of the radical character of integral ecology can be found in the critique of the technocratic paradigm. This paradigm is influenced by 'the idea of infinite or unlimited growth which proves to be so attractive to economists, financiers, and experts in technology' (*LS*, 106). This outlook in turn 'is based on the lie that there is an infinite supply of the earth's goods and thus leads to the planet being squeezed dry' (*LS*, 106). The myth of endless growth, development and progress must be abandoned. There is a slow, but gradual, dawning that the status quo of business and finance can no longer continue. In a frank interview, Mark Carney, head of the Bank of England, on the BBC4 *Today* programme, issued a warning that the world will face irreversible heating unless firms shift their priorities. He pointed out that the financial sector has begun to curb investment in fossil fuels – but far too slowly. He notes that the risks associated with an increase of 4 degrees centigrade will effect a nine-metre rise in sea levels, searing heatwaves, droughts and serious food supply problems.[13] These words of warning from someone at the centre of the capitalist system are a wake-up call for everyone.

On the other hand, it needs to be pointed out that calls for the promotion of 'sustainable development', while seeming to support ecological change, need to be treated with some caution. Integral ecology is not about promoting 'sustainable development'. This new rhetoric of 'sustainable development' needs to be scrutinised carefully. More often than not, this new popular slogan is often a coded way of maintaining the status quo with just a few tweaks here and there. The concept of 'sustainable development' goes back to a report put out by the United Nations, in association with the World Bank, entitled *Our Common Future: The World Commission on Environment and Development* (1987). This report seeks to overcome tensions between economic growth and ecological stability. According to some commentators, the concept is highly ambiguous, conceptually vague and open to manipulation. All too often, and sometimes unwittingly, 'sustainable development' is about maintaining sustainable economic growth rather than reforming the causes of ecological degradation.[14]

This manipulation of 'sustainable development' into sustaining the economic status quo helps us to understand a remark in *Querida Amazonia*, which points out that 'an integral ecology cannot be content simply with fine-tuning technical questions or political, juridical and social decisions. The best ecology always has an educational dimension that can encourage the development of new habits in individuals and groups.'[15]

What this means in effect is that the concept of integral ecology commits us to realising that climate change is connected to economics, healthcare, migration, food supplies and politics. Ecology, therefore, is not an external add-on with dimensions of life, but is, rather, intrinsic to the whole of life.

This overview of the radical meaning of integral ecology demands a renewal of theology if it is to enter into serious dialogue with ecology. Is theology up to this new challenge? Does theology have a vision that will animate engagement in an inter-disciplinary dialogue with ecology?

Ecology and the Renewal of Theology

If it is true that integral ecology requires an integrated, trans-disciplinary approach, it is also equally true that integral ecology has far-reaching consequences for the way we do theology in the twenty-first century. Theology cannot stand by and watch the transformation required of other disciplines without putting its own house in order. Ecology must interrogate the way theology is done. Equally, theology must engage critically and constructively with ecology.

As *Laudato Si'* points out: 'Given the complexity of the ecological crisis and its multiple causes, we need to realise that solutions will not emerge just from one way of interpreting and transforming reality' (*LS*, 63). Rather, 'respect must be shown for various cultural riches of different people, their art and poetry, their interior life and spirituality' (*LS*, 63). In effect, 'no branch of the sciences and no form of wisdom can be left out, and that includes religion and the language particular to it' (*LS*, 63). It should be remembered that *Laudato Si'* is addressed to the whole of humanity, and not just Christians. For that reason, the encyclical does not construct an ecological theology, lest that alienate non-believers. Rightly, it leaves the task of reconstructing theology to the community of theologians. However, *Laudato Si'* is making a clear case for a two-way conversation between ecology and theology.

Ecology will challenge theology to move into a more integrated paradigm, to explain the meaning of dominion in Genesis 1, and to foster a new praxis dedicated to the healing of the planet. Equally, theology will challenge ecology to move from an anthropocentric approach to a theocentric approach, to make way for the cultivation of beauty in our world, and to give priority to hearing the cry of the poor and the earth. How theology might engage in this two-way conversation is only hinted at here and there in *Laudato Si'*, yet it must be acknowledged that the ecological emergency has huge implications for the way theology is done and understands itself in the twenty-first century. This radical shift has already begun to take place through, for example, the establishment of the Earth Bible Project in Exeter in the UK, through the outline of what is called ecological hermeneutics, and through the establishment of *Laudato Si'* institutes in the US, the UK, the EU and Latin American countries. These initiatives have generated some controversy, but the broad principles are to be welcomed and refined within a mutually critical engagement between theology and ecology.

The late Australian eco-theologian, Denis Edwards, suggests that '*Laudato Si'* sets an agenda for the church and the world that is of such importance that it must also be a dialogue partner for Systematic theologians now and into the future'.[16] Theologian Celia Deane-Drummond notes that 'the theological dimension is woven throughout the encyclical', and then goes on to say that 'these underlying theological elements are vital in order to appreciate the rich underlying tapestry that motivates this encyclical'.[17] Elizabeth Johnson points out that when we realise the importance of the conversation between ecology and theology then it will be necessary for church liturgies and eucharistic prayers, religious art and music, preaching and teaching, to take account of the ecological challenge.[18] Columban priest and theologian Seán McDonagh was quick to point out that *Laudato Si'* is not only about climate change but also, and equally importantly, about the destruction of biodiversity. McDonagh emphasises that the loss of biodiversity 'has enormous implications for Christian living in our world today'.[19] Up to now, most attention has, rightly, been given to the development of environmental ethics. It is now time to complement environmental ethics by expounding the theological foundations of the encyclical in greater detail.

In other words, *Laudato Si'* calls for a new way of doing theology. In the light of what the encyclical says about integral ecology, theology needs to change from the bottom up. It will need to be more inductive, attending to the data of experience, discerning the action of the Spirit in creation, in history, in Christian communities and in the religions of the world.

The following chapters seek to initiate a new dialogue between ecology and theology by focusing on fundamental questions like anthropology, pneumatology, Christology, eschatology, liturgy and eucharist. One could have chosen other dialogue-partners such as ecclesiology, sacramentality, morality, grace, ecumenism or inter-faith engagement. This book concentrates on the first six areas listed above because they are foundational to everything else and, in a sense, are presupposed in the latter six areas listed. In opting for foundational themes, personal assumptions, social imaginaries and cosmic paradigms that have been operative in the way theology has been done up to now will have to be questioned. This new direction should help us to look critically at the world of ecology to discover some forgotten ancient truths such as:

- Matter reveals Spirit
- The secular mediates the sacred
- The human images the divine
- Nature discloses grace
- Creation is sacramental

Further, it is hoped that theology will go beyond the traditional understanding of salvation as something exclusive to humans to include and embrace redemption of the earth community as part of the redemption of humanity.

On 29 January 2018, after the publication of *Laudato Si'*, Pope Francis published a follow-up document calling for 'radical' reform of theology, entitled 'An Apostolic Constitution on Ecclesiastical Universities and Faculties', *Veritatis Gaudium*. This document proposes a significant reform of the conduct of theology in pontifical universities. It takes account of the pastoral implications of *Laudato Si'* for faith seeking understanding.

This eighty-seven-page document begins by noting: 'There is a need to acknowledge the changed social-cultural context' in which theology takes place today. We are living not only in a time of change, but we are also experiencing 'a true epochal shift, marked by wide-ranging anthropological and environmental crises.'[20] Further, the document refers to 'the natural, social and financial disasters which are swiftly reaching a breaking point'.[21] This requires 'changing the models of global development and redefining our notion of progress'. Pontifical theological faculties constitute a 'sort of providential cultural laboratory in which the Church carries out a performative interpretation of the reality brought about by the Christ event.'[22]

In view of this, a 'radical paradigm shift' and a 'bold cultural revolution' are required to meet these new needs.[23] This would involve the establishment of world networks of ecclesiastical universities and faculties to promote the Gospel and the Church tradition which are, at the same time, 'open to new situations and ideas'. This renewal of theology will be fruitful 'only if it is done with an open mind and on one's knees'. It is pointed out that 'the theologian who is satisfied with his complete and conclusive thought is mediocre', whereas 'the good theologian and philosopher has an open, that is an incomplete, thought, always open to the *maius* of God and of the truth, always in development'.[24]

The document offers four criteria for theological studies that are rooted in the teaching of the Second Vatican Council and inspired by the changes that have taken place since then. The first criterion is about 'the contemplation and presentation of a spiritual, intellectual, and existential introduction to ... the *Kerygma* and the Good News of Jesus Christ'.[25] The second criterion is about the need for a 'wide-ranging dialogue', which is a 'requirement for experiencing in community the joy of the truth'.[26] The third criterion is the need for 'interdisciplinary and cross-disciplinary approaches' to be carried out 'with wisdom and creativity in the light of Revelation'.[27] What is distinctive about theological studies is 'the vital intellectual principle of the unity in difference of knowledge and respect for its multiple, correlated, and convergent expressions'.[28] The fourth criterion is about the need for 'net-working' and 'co-operation' among theological faculties.

Under 'Norms', it is worth noting that the document talks about evangelisation and the presentation of the truths of the faith 'in a manner adapted to various cultures'.[29]

This document was followed by a second statement on theology, entitled 'Theology after *Veritatis Gaudium* in the Context of the Mediterranean'. This was a key-note address by Pope Francis to the Pontifical Theological Faculty of southern Italy, Naples, on 21 June 2019. At the time some described the address as an international landmark. The document begins by addressing the question under review in the following way: 'I would say that theology, particularly in this context (that is the Mediterranean context) is called to be a welcoming theology'. This requires 'developing a sincere dialogue with social and civil institutions, with universities and research centres … for the construction in peace of an inclusive society, and also for the care of creation'. The document goes on to explain that: 'Dialogue … is the hallmark of a theology of acceptance'. The document suggests that dialogue is a 'double movement: a movement from below towards the "On-High" through listening and discernment'. At the same time, dialogue also includes 'a movement from the "On-High" (Jesus on the Cross) towards the below to discern the signs of God in history'. Of particular note is the call for 'a theological Pentecost', which allows men and women to hear 'in their own native language' the Christian message that responds to their search for meaning. For this to happen, there must be theological freedom: 'Without the possibility of experiencing new paths, nothing new is created, and there is no place for the newness of the Spirit of the Risen One'. The document criticises those who 'long for a monolithic body of doctrine guarded by all and leaving no room for nuance'. One of the themes running through this address at Naples is the emphasis on the Spirit, listening to, and discerning what the Spirit is saying at this time in history.

The significance of these two documents is wide-ranging. It is clear that they were written in support of the theological implications of *Laudato Si'* and to encourage theologians to rise to the challenges of engaging with ecology. The documents change the atmosphere in which theology is done, so that it is done in the service of humanity, the care of Mother Earth and in an interdisciplinary engagement with ecology. The documents encourage theologians to explore new frontiers in this new 'epochal' moment. They challenge theologians to engage with other disciplines. They shift the emphasis from orthodoxy to ortho-praxis. They call for a reading of the signs of the times in the spirit of the Second Vatican Council. In brief, these two documents herald the dawn of a new era in the praxis of faith seeking understanding in the service of the care of our common home.

One of the many implications arising from these two documents is that theology in the future will have to engage more constructively and critically with science. It is not surprising therefore that *Laudato Si'* calls for 'an intense dialogue' between religion and science that can be 'fruitful for both' (*LS*, 62).

Dialogue between Theology and Science

There has been a stand-off between theology and science over the centuries, conditioned by the conflicts between the Church and scientists in the past. This stand-off gave rise to the creation of stereotypes on both sides, to the diminishment of the self-understanding of theology and science. The stand-off began to change in the middle of the last century. Ian Barbur, among others, outlined the possibility of four different ways of conceiving the relationship that might exist between theology and science: conflict, integration, independence and dialogue. The model of dialogue has come to the fore in the light of the Second Vatican Council, especially the *Gaudium et Spes* (*Pastoral Constitution on the Church in the Modern World*).[30] A helpful context in which to locate the dialogue between theology and science is the long-standing relationship within Christianity between faith and reason. This goes back to Augustine, is developed by Aquinas, affirmed by the Second Vatican Council and present in the teaching of recent popes. This tradition sees faith and reason as complementary, rather than conflictual, though of course there will be moments of tension as theology seeks a middle way between fideism and rationalism. The Second Vatican Council takes up this relationship between faith and reason and applies it explicitly to the relationship that should exist between the Church and the world. The Church has much to learn from the modern world, and the modern world has something to learn from the Church.[31] The council developed an important principle of the mutuality that can and should exist between the Church and the world. There is no reason why this model of mutuality, of critical and constructive dialogue, should not inform and shape the relationship between theology and science in the twenty-first century.

A good example of this relationship between theology and science can be found in some of the writings of John Paul II. In a significant 'Message' to the Director of the Vatican Observatory on 1 June 1998,

John Paul II raised a number of important questions for the dialogue between theology and science. Among the issues of interest were:

> Might contemporary cosmology have something to offer to our reflection on creation?

> Does an evolutionary perspective bring any light to bear upon theological anthropology?

> What, if any, are the eschatological implications of contemporary cosmology, especially in the light of the vast future of our universe?[32]

Having raised these questions, he goes on to say:

> Science can purify religion from error and superstition; religion can purify science from idolatry and false absolutes. Each can draw the other into a wider world.[33]

In a second letter to the Pontifical Academy of Science, John Paul II stated that: 'new findings lead us towards a recognition of evolution as more than just a hypothesis'.[34]

These questions and statements by John Paul II have opened up the way for a critical and constructive dialogue between theology and science, and this dialogue in turn paves the way for serious engagement between ecology and theology. One of the lessons emerging from this relationship between theology and science is that theology has become more refined, nuanced and circumspect in its statements about the action of the Spirit of God in the world. For instance, theology now recognises that God is not an object alongside other objects, not an item of information alongside other items of information, not an explanation alongside other explanations, not a cause alongside other causes. If God were merely any one of these, then people would lose interest very quickly, and this may well be the reason why so many *are* losing interest. Another lesson from the dialogue between theology and science is this: It needs to be stated that the God of contemporary faith does not intervene externally from time to time in the natural processes of biological evolution and developments within history. Instead, the God of the Judaeo-Christian tradition is a God who is already involved in the world from the beginning through the gift of the Spirit poured out on creation and all flesh.[35] This gift of the Spirit continues to be active intrinsically in the world in surprising ways: in creation and history, in biological evolution, in the findings of modern science, through the extraordinary advances of the modern sciences through powerful microscopes and telescopes, in the awakening of the inner life and the experience of transcendence within human beings.

A third lesson is that we need to be clear that, according to theology, faith in God is not a blind leap in the dark; instead, it is a reasoned response of the whole person embracing the movements of experience, trust, joy, emotions, desire, moral sensibilities, imagination and interpretation. These different experiences are often stirred and awakened by the wonders of the universe disclosed by the findings of physics, cosmology and biological evolution. The experience of God is more about God finding us than us finding God. To this extent, the revelation of God in human experience is not a projection, but a discovery of what is already there; it is not merely a human creation, but the unravelling of a gift already given; it is not an invention, but a making explicit of what we already know implicitly and are vaguely familiar with. On the other hand, the experience of God is not some kind of exotic, out-of-body experience; instead it is often an experience of the most ordinary kind that takes on extraordinary religious, even mystical, signification. A fourth lesson is that theology needs to learn how to approach the Mystery of God revealed in the Christ-event in a spirit of humility. This means discovering that the more we say about God, the more likely it is that we will get God wrong. Loose talk about God often ends up not edifying people, but generating, unwittingly, new forms of atheism, incredulity and alienation. In contrast, theology must acknowledge, with humility, that we know very little about God, and that, more often than not, 'less is more' when it comes to talking about the Mystery of God. This means that theology needs a new appreciation of the value of 'learned ignorance' (*docta ignorantia*) as a form of knowledge, and begins to realise that such ignorance is the beginning of theological wisdom. At the same time, however, before we can arrive at this 'learned ignorance', we have to plumb the depths of the historical and personal revelation of God in Jesus Christ. The originality of that revelation is that 'God is love',[36] an insight that unfolded in the New Testament and the early centuries in terms of understanding the One God as Father, Son and Spirit *and* as Spirit, Son and Father. Communicating the uniqueness of the Christ-event for ecology will require an expansion of the theological imagination in a way that is able to engage with other religions as intimated by the Second Vatican Council. Only then can we move to the cultivation of a fully informed 'learned ignorance'. At the same time, it needs to be noted that there is nothing more destructive of theology, and of the dialogue between theology and science, than a premature negative theology. As Pope Francis has cautioned, theology must be careful not to reduce God to 'a magician, with a wand, able to do everything. But this is not so.'[37]

On the other hand, the questions raised by John Paul II, and endorsed by Francis, require a mutually illuminating dialogue between theology and science that can challenge theology to engage creatively with the science of ecology. For example, how can theology, conscious of its own limitations, continue to talk meaningfully about God in the face of the many challenges posed by the scientific theory of evolution? Is it possible to construct a theology of creation that does not clash with, or contradict, the scientific theory of evolution? Is there room for God within evolution, without lapsing into a new 'god of the gaps'? There are many theologies of creation seeking to do just that, and this question continues to be on the agenda in the ongoing dialogue between theology and science. One response to this question is put forward by Karl Rahner. According to Rahner, God's self-communication to the world is what effects creation. In that originating act of the self-communication of God, the universe was endowed with the gift of self-transcendence. This dynamic of self-transcendence exists throughout creation: it is mirrored in the expanding cosmology, in the surprises of evolution, in the restlessness of the human spirit. As such, this gift of self-transcendence enables the emergence of the new within the course of history. The whole of creation is gifted through the action of the Spirit with a capacity for self-transcendence, and is endowed from the beginning with an impulse towards creativity.

It is this gift of self-transcendence, implanted *ab initio*, through the self-bestowal of God in creation, that enables creation to become more than it is. This is possible because God is present through the movement from the Big Bang through to an expanding cosmos, to biological evolution, and to the historical emergence of self-conscious human beings. This proposal from Rahner begs another question: how can we attribute to this divine presence the existence of massive amounts of death and destruction along the way? In acknowledging the value of Rahner's presentation, the late Denis Edwards (1943–2019) notes that Rahner's view 'needs to be linked more fully to Pneumatology',[38] a suggestion taken up in Chapter 3 of this book.

Another area where progress has been made in the dialogue between theology and science is the new appreciation or, more accurately, the deeper appreciation of matter. Matter is not the exclusive domain of science. Theology affirms the value and depth of matter as the *locus* of the divine through the indwelling of the Spirit at the dawn of time, and the Word becoming flesh/matter in Jesus. This particular point will be addressed in Chapter 4.

Another area of common interest in the dialogue between theology and science is the turn to hermeneutics. Theology and science, each in their own way, depend on the use of metaphors, models and paradigms. This, in turn, raises the question of the role of hermeneutics, the art of interpreting the data of human experience and the evidence from the laboratory, in and through metaphors, models and paradigms. This question of the role of hermeneutics is of central importance to the dialogue between theology and science. As far back as the nineteenth century, Friedrich Nietzsche disturbed the worlds of theology and science with the challenging sound-bite: 'There are no facts, only interpretations'. The turn to hermeneutics, with the help of the philosophy of science, reveals that science, in spite of its claims to be detached and objective, may nonetheless be driven by underlying subjective considerations, like the quest for meaning, the search for order, the pursuit of beauty and a passion for truth, not to mention less noble motives. There is no such thing as a value-free, neutral interpretation. Likewise, theology is discovering, through the turn to hermeneutics, that it must continually check its subjective dispositions against the objective realities of history, texts and traditions. In other words, it is increasingly clear, in the light of hermeneutics, that the hard sciences may have a soft centre, and the so-called soft sciences of theology may have a hard edge to them. If it is true to say that interpretation is a key to theology and science, it must also be acknowledged that interpretation itself is closely connected to the exercise of a disciplined human imagination. This remark can sometimes make scientists and theologians a little edgy, when their enterprises become associated with the exercise of imagination. And yet, it may be in the areas of interpretation *and imagination* that the most interesting debates and progress will take place in the future in the dialogue between faith and science, and especially in the conversation between theology and ecology. It should be borne in mind that both science and theology talk quite extensively about unobservable entities, yet the only way of doing this is in and through the creative power of imagination. The real challenge facing theology and science in the future will be about invoking imagination in a manner that promotes the freedom and flourishing not only of human beings but also of the wider community of creation.

CHAPTER 2

Theological Anthropology and Integral Ecology

ANTHROPOLOGY IS a highly contested area right across a range of disciplines in contemporary thought: ecology, ethics, economics, education, feminism, gender studies, philosophy and theology. Once you go below the surface of any of these areas, you will find underlying assumptions at play about what it means to be human. To illustrate the point, in 2016, Jeffrey Sachs, US economist and UN adviser, gave a keynote address to the London School of Economics on 'Subjective well-being over the life course'. In his opening remarks, he pointed out that 'economics went widely off the track by a profoundly flawed model of human nature and a flawed model of human purpose'[1]. In an 'Introduction' to his short book *Being Human: Bodies, Minds, Persons* (2018) Rowan Williams suggests, in restrained fashion: 'There are grounds for being a bit concerned about our current models of human life and human well-being.'[2] The reflections in this chapter will be limited to the dominant influence of anthropology on ecology and theology.

Anthropology is the study of what it means to be a human being, an examination of what is at stake at the core of human identity, an analysis of what promotes human flourishing and an exploration of human nature in the light of the social sciences, history, philosophy and theology. The surest sign of a deep crisis in anthropology is the contemporary inability to talk seriously about death in the public forum. At this time in the context of a climate emergency, a dialogue between anthropology and ecology is urgent, especially since the behaviour of human beings is the cause of the increasing collapse of eco-systems.

There are a number of questions that ecology will ask of theology in the context of anthropology. It will begin by requesting theology to correct those teachings in the Christian tradition that have given rise to anthropocentrism. In particular, ecology will seek a reinterpretation of the biblical injunction to have 'dominion' over the creatures of the earth and to 'subdue' the earth (Genesis 1:26 and 28). In this context, ecology will critique the instrumentalisation of nature that has followed from this biblical injunction. Ecology will also ask theology to analyse the negative impact of anthropocentrism on so many areas of Christian life: relationships, roles, reductionist perceptions of the natural world, and the human-centred doctrine of salvation. Ecology will also invite theology to be more inductive and particular in its claims before moving towards universal principles.

On the other hand, theology will seek the help of ecology in the reconstruction of anthropology in a way that gives due weight to a balanced relationship between the human and the natural world. Theology will also ask ecology to keep an open space for the presence of divine transcendence within the emerging new ecological paradigm, without introducing a new 'God of the gaps'. Theology will also seek the help of ecology in relocating the life of the human within the life of nature without conflating the two.

There is a growing awareness that anthropocentrism is a major cause of the ecological crisis. An anthropology that puts man at the front and centre of everything has been found to be wanting on many fronts. It is the source of the alienation of human beings from the natural world. It is the justification for a reckless, self-centred instrumentalisation of nature. It is also a cause of a reductionist understanding of the natural world that construes it as a 'lifeless object' available for exploitation.

As far back as 1967, Lynn White, a medieval historian, pointed out that the anthropocentric Judaeo-Christian faiths were responsible for the modern 'ecologic crisis'.[3] Around the same time, Thomas Berry, a Passionist priest, describing himself as a 'geologian', was highlighting the need for humans as a species 'to reimagine and reinvent themselves'[4] in the light of the emerging ecological crisis.

Critique of Anthropocentrism

If the human is a major part of the problem within the ecological crisis, then the human must become also part of the solution. It is increasingly clear that the self-understanding of the human must change, but the relationship, or, more accurately, the lack of a recognition of the deep relationship between the human and the world of nature must also be remedied. Anthropocentrism has permeated the whole of theology since the late Middle Ages, especially in the areas of grace, salvation and eschatology. This has led to a neglect of the cosmic dimension of these areas. Elizabeth A. Johnson notes how 'over the centuries ... theology narrowed its interests to focus on human beings almost exclusively', and this in turn resulted in the presence of 'a powerful anthropocentric paradigm' that shaped everything else.[5] Dan Horan points to the existence of an 'anthropocentric privilege' that has had the effect of excluding the non-human world as part of the image of God and thereby granting a licence to humans for dominion over non-human creation.[6] David G. Kirchhoffer challenges theology to overcome the presence of an 'egoistic anthropocentric' understanding of existence that has diminished our appreciation of the natural world.[7] Neil Ormerod and Christina Vanin talk about the existence of a 'hyper-anthropological culture' which has legitimed the domination of the natural order in a way that inhibits ecological conversion because it cuts off the human from cosmological meaning and alienates them from the rhythms and cycles of nature.[8]

One author who has given a compelling analysis of the rise and rise of anthropocentrism is the Canadian philosopher Charles Taylor. The value of Taylor's account of anthropocentrism is that he locates it within a gradual shift over five hundred years from belief to unbelief. Only a selective sketch can be given here of Taylor's contributions. Our filter will be Taylor's take on anthropology and how it helps us today to understand the alienation of the self from the natural world. Taylor outlines this in a major work entitled *A Secular Age* (2007), which draws on part of a previous volume, *Sources of the Self* (1989).

According to Taylor, we have moved from a situation in which faith was the norm to one in which unbelief is the new norm for an ever-increasing number of people. This did not happen overnight. Instead, it took place gradually under the weight of the Enlightenment, the rise of modernity and the emerging process of secularisation. Within this process, there was a shift from a transcendent frame of reference to a purely immanent frame of reference. Some transcendent frames attributed miracles to divine intervention and sacred texts to divine dictation. Immanent frames increasingly explained miracles away as being natural events with natural causes we simply do not yet understand, and attributed sacred texts solely to the work of their human authors. This shift produced the rise of an exclusive humanism which led to the development of a disenchanted universe, and a perception of the cosmos as impersonal in 'the most forbidding sense, blind and indifferent to our fate'.[9] At the centre of this shift over a period of five hundred years is the shaping and reshaping of the human self. In this regard, Taylor describes the pre-modern self as 'porous' (open) and the modern self as 'buffered' (enclosed). The pre-modern 'porous' self was open to spirits, cosmic forces and transcendent influences. In contrast, the modern self is an 'enclosed' self, with a wall between itself and the world. The modern self is disengaged from the natural world, disembedded from society and disenchanted with the universe. This 'buffered' self is cut off from any transcendent horizon and stands alone within an immanent frame of self-sufficiency.

To complete this account of anthropology we need to move beyond Taylor to say something briefly about the post-modern critique of the modern self. Not all is well with the self-sufficient subject of modernity. For some post-moderns, the modern self is just a rhetorical flourish that facilitates transactions of power and desire. Richard Rorty sums up this position about the modern self when he says: 'There is nothing deep down inside [the self] except what we put there ourselves.'[10] Another post-modern, Michel Foucault, says that modern man is a recent invention that will disappear like a drawing in the sand.[11] There are small grains of truth in Rorty and Foucault that will be taken up in an attempt to reconstruct anthropology in the service of an ecological culture. For the moment, it is sufficient to see the link between the modern self and the rise of anthropocentrism, and the alienation it causes of the human from the natural world and the cosmos.

This modern alienation of the human from nature is largely responsible for the ecological crisis. The separation of the human from the natural world has given modern man licence to engage with nature as a lifeless object, available for endless exploitation as if it were infinite. The natural world has become an inert site for dumping technological and industrial waste.[12] Further, this alienation of the human from the natural world has resulted in a highly utilitarian approach to nature, denying it any intrinsic value. Nature has come to be seen as a machine, devoid of symbolic content, available for exploitation and the profit of some.

Another important critique of anthropocentrism comes from eco-feminism.[13] Mary Doak points out that as far back as 1970 a link was established by Rosemary R. Ruether between patriarchy and the oppression of women, and the exploitation of eco-systems. Eco-feminism points to parallels between the exploitation of women and the exploitation of the earth. The domination of women by men is reflected in the male exploitation of the earth. The way the female body is objectified mirrors the way the body of the earth is objectified.

Lying behind these different forms of exploitation is the presence of what some call hierarchical dualisms, and others refer to as binary systems of thought underpinning the presence of so much anthropocentrism in theology. These dualisms are found in the division between spirit and matter, soul and body, person and nature, mind and flesh. Such binaries have been used to devalue women in relation to men, the body in relation to the soul, matter in relation to the spirit and the natural world in relation to patriarchy. These binaries run deep and are often reflected in the divide between scientific reason and human emotion.

A new paradigm is required to transform these dualisms. A first step would be the construction of a theology of radical relationality, reaching across the natural world and human beings. At the centre of this theology of relationality would be the role of the human community as the primary source of identity. This community would foster a sense of mutuality, reciprocity and equality within relationships.

A second step would be the development of a theology of embodiment, the embodiment of the person and the embodiment of the earth. This would require close attention to the dynamics of human experience, recognising that all experience is embodied and that, therefore, the representation and interpretation of experiences are the prerogative of the one having the experience.

A third step would be to adopt Teilhard de Chardin's principle around the unity of spirit and matter. According to Teilhard, there is no such thing as matter and no such thing as spirit; instead there is only spirit-matter in the universe. The next section will look at these suggestions when mapping out some elements in the reconstruction of anthropology.

To complete this critique of anthropocentrism it may be helpful to see what *Laudato Si'* has to say about the presence of anthropocentrism in the modern world. It is worth noting that Chapter 3 of the encyclical is devoted to 'The Human Roots of the Ecological Crisis'; within this chapter, there is a sub-section entitled 'The Crisis and Effects of Modern Anthropocentrism' (*LS*, 115–21). The encyclical establishes two key principles for the construction of a new anthropology. On the one hand, it affirms:

> There can be no renewal of our relationship with nature without a renewal of humanity. (*LS*, 118)

On the other hand, the encyclical states:

> There can be no ecology without an adequate anthropology. (*LS*, 118)

The modern self-understanding of the human is at the centre of the ecological crisis. It is primarily human beings who have to change their self-understanding if there is to be a more balanced and integrated relationship between the human and ecology. The encyclical distinguishes different forms of anthropocentrism. The first is what it calls 'modern anthropocentrism' (*LS*, 115). This outlook is influenced by a technical approach to nature which is seen as 'an insensate order … a cold body of facts … a mere given … an object of utility … raw material to be hammered into a useful shape' (*LS*, 115). Further, this outlook sees 'the cosmos … as mere "space" into which objects can be thrown with complete indifference' and, therefore, the 'intrinsic dignity of the world is compromised' (*LS*, 115). Taken from Romano Guardini, this statement captures a modern mindset that is all too often evident in the mining industry and in fossil fuel corporations.

A second misrepresentation of the human is called 'excessive anthropocentrism' (*LS*, 116). This form of anthropocentrism neglects the importance of 'social bonds', ignores 'the limits' of reality, and is influenced by 'a promethean vision of mastery over the world'. This outlook, in some instances, goes back to a particular interpretation of the biblical injunction to have 'dominion' over the earth and to 'fill and keep it' (Genesis 1:28) which the encyclical admits was incorrect and needs to be corrected today (*LS*, 67).

A third misunderstanding of the human is described as 'tyrannical anthropocentrism' (*LS*, 68). This approach ignores the biblical emphasis on relationships, not only among individuals, but also with other living beings (*LS*, 68). Further, tyrannical anthropocentrism is 'unconcerned for other creatures' (*LS*, 68).

A final form of misrepresenting the human is described as 'misguided anthropocentrism' (*LS*, 118, 119, 122) This view arises 'when human beings place themselves at the centre', giving 'priority to immediate convenience' (*LS*, 122). This fourth misunderstanding of the human 'underestimates the importance of interpersonal relations' and 'openness to others' (*LS*, 119). This review of different forms of anthropocentrism puts down markers for the reconstruction of anthropology in the service of ecology. These markers include:

- the need to recover the relational character of the natural world;
- the importance of respect for the dignity and value of nature in itself;
- the working out of a new relationship between the human and nature;
- a recognition of the place of interpersonal relations within community.

The Reconstruction of Anthropology in the Service of Ecology

There is widespread agreement that anthropology needs to be reconfigured from the ground up, and from the inside out. This reconstruction of the human is required in the light of the new cosmic story, the presence of so much man-made ecological destruction, and the sharp divisions within society around male and female identity. To begin to address these challenges, we will look at the human in the light of 'Big History', how personal relationships are formed and the complex network of relationships that exist within nature.

One of the key insights and benefits of 'Big History/Deep Time' is the existence of an underlying unity and relationship between cosmology, evolutionary biology and the emergence of the human. According to scientists, the universe came into being from the flaring forth of a singular event some fourteen billion years ago. From within that singularity there arose an unfolding and expanding cosmology, out of which came the earth and from which issued the evolution of biological life. Out of that life, there emerged the existence of human beings some 200,000 years ago. It should be noted that this story is the favoured scientific explanation of the origins of the universe available at this time. This scientific theory should not be confused or identified with the biblical theology of creation. Instead, we are dealing here with two different accounts of the world, the one being the science of cosmology and the other being a theological account of the origins and development of the universe in terms of creation.

Within 'Big History' we can speak symbolically about the human as cosmic dust in a state of consciousness, made up of the matter of stars. The British scientist and theologian, Arthur Peacocke, liked to remind his students: 'Every atom in our blood would not be there had it not been produced by some galactic explosion billions of years ago and eventually condensed to form the iron in the crust of the earth from which we have emerged'.[14] According to some, the universe expanded the way it did because it was coded from the beginning to support life. This theory is known as the 'Anthropic Principle'. It is a view that is by no means accepted by all scientists, but nonetheless remains fascinating in the context of anthropology. Stage one of 'Big History' is the Big Bang that initiated the story of the universe, giving rise to a movement from matter to life, and from life to human consciousness. Many scientists agree that we live in a finely tuned universe; according to Stephen Hawking, 'If the rate of expansion one second after the Big Bang had been smaller by even one part of a hundred thousand million million, the universe would have recollapsed before it reached its present size'.[15] The human disregard of this fine-tuning in relation to the earth's systems is largely responsible for the ecological crisis today. Stage two of the universe story is about the significant evolution of biological life on earth out of the expanding cosmology. Here a remarkable shift from matter to biological life takes place. Stage three is about the evolutionary emergence and creation of the human out of biological life. What distinguishes human life from biological life is the presence, within the human, of reflective self-consciousness, the development of a sophisticated linguistic system as a means of communication and the creative capacity of the human to imagine the past and anticipate the future.

Holmes Rolston talks about three Big Bangs that should be taken into account in trying to understand who we are: the Big Bang of cosmology, the Big Bang of the biological evolution of life and the Big Bang of the emergence of reflective self-consciousness. Within these three Big Bangs, there is an underlying continuum from one stage to the next. At the same time there are astounding 'jumps' from matter to life and from life to mind. Within these 'jumps' there are surprising transformations and unpredictable outcomes. There is the presence, on the one hand, of continuity within and on the other hand a radical discontinuity. How then are we to understand this identity-within-transformation within the cosmic story? How can we begin to understand the epic of evolution from the inside out, as well as the outside in? Is there something going on in the inside that is not visible on the outside? In trying to answer these questions, we can glean some light from Teilhard de Chardin and Thomas Berry.

According to Teilhard, there is an inside and an outside to the whole of reality. The inside he calls 'interiority' and it is found explicitly in human beings in and through the different levels of self-consciousness. If there is an interiority within the human, then we can ask the question: is it not possible that there may be some degree of interiority, or something resembling 'interiority' within the rest of reality? For Teilhard

> It is a fact, beyond question, that deep within ourselves we
> can discern, as though through a rent, an 'interior' at the heart
> of things; and this glimpse is sufficient to force upon us the

conviction that in one degree or another this 'interior' exists and has always existed in nature.[16]

Teilhard develops this theme of the 'within' and 'without' of things, the inner and outer dimension of reality, in terms of the unity that exists between spirit and matter. For Teilhard

There is neither spirit nor matter in the world; the stuff of the universe is spirit-matter. No other subject but this could produce the human molecule.[17]

What is important in the context of the search for an adequate anthropology is that Teilhard suggests some form of interiority exists, not only explicitly in the human, but also to some degree 'in nature'.

A similar suggestion can be found in Thomas Berry, who would have been influenced, in some respects, by Teilhard de Chardin. Whereas Teilhard talks about the interiority of things, Berry posits the presence of subjectivity within the story of evolution. In a well-known quotation, Berry points out that

The universe is not a collection of objects but a communion of subjects.[18]

For Berry, within evolution there are different degrees of subjectivity, and this means, in effect, that there is some form of subjectivity within nature. Firstly, this emphasis on interiority and subjectivity within nature is important for ecology in terms of relocating the human within nature, and not as outside of nature. Secondly, this presence of interiority and subjectivity within nature is an important bridge in re-establishing the bond between the human and the natural world. Thirdly, this focus on the 'within' of nature engenders a sense of empathy with, and responsibility for, nature by human beings.

Against this background of the new cosmic story, and the underlying unity between nature and human beings, we can now look more closely at the development and formation of the human as radically relational. The profile of the human has been changing in the light of the new cosmic story and the growing awareness of the damage being done by man-made climate change. It is necessary to move from the self-centred individualism of modern anthropocentrism to a more dynamic, relational and inter-personal view of the human. We do not come into the world with a ready-made identity; instead, we leave the world with an identity shaped and influenced by encounters with others. We are not individual persons who may or may not have relationships with others. We are, rather, persons only in relation to others. We become persons as members of a community. We become who we are only in and through relations that begin from conception onwards.

Another way of saying this is to move from Descartes' influential 'I think, therefore, I am' towards an anthropology that recognises, first of all, that 'we are' before 'I am', or, as one African proverb puts it: 'We relate, therefore, I am'. Teilhard, reflecting on evolution, observes that what comes first is not individual being, but union, which gives rise to relational being. Being is first a 'we', before it can become an 'I'. To exist, therefore, is always to co-exist; to be is to be in relationships; being (*esse*) is always being towards (*esse ad*). From beginning to end, human beings are constituted by relationships with others and the community to which we belong. We come into the world out of a relationship into a situation of relational dependence and most likely will leave the world in a relationship of dependency. If this is the case, can it be consistent to abandon our relationality between beginnings and endings? Can we know who we are by ignoring the vast network of complex relationships that surround us in nature and society?

One way of moving towards a radical relationality of personhood is to look briefly at the African philosophy of *Ubuntu*. *Ubuntu* is a Nguni term meaning a way of being that is summed up in the expression 'I am because we are'. The focus here is on what it means to be human. The human becomes a person through other persons. The person is actualised in relating to others: it is in and through the experience of being together that we become human. Being human is as much an ongoing project as it is a reality. We do not become an individual human being in isolation, but rather in relation to others and, in particular, by becoming part of the community: being human is a social project. At the centre of Ubuntu philosophy is the importance of mutual respect,

41

dignity and compassion as integral elements in the project of being human together in community.[19]

To sum up this critique of anthropocentrism, it can be said that at the centre of twentieth-century culture there stands the shining, self-sufficient subject of modernity. This subject has given rise to rugged, aggressive and competitive forms of individualism. Under these forms of individualism human beings have felt free to act as they like, without much regard for other human beings, even less regard for non-human creatures, and still less for the interior life of the earth. In effect, this kind of individualism has lost touch with others, with community values, the need for any kind of communion among other human beings, and the larger community of creation. The effects of this kind of modern individualism are far-reaching from an ecological point of view. They include:

- the alienation of the human from the natural world;
- the legitimation of exploitative attitudes and practices towards nature;
- the isolation of the individual from the community of creation;
- the de-sacralisation of nature;
- the dis-enchantment of the universe.

Expanding the Dynamic of Interpersonal Relations

How then do we negotiate this radically relational character of the human? It is not enough to say that as persons we are constituted by relationships. To be a relational person involves being a person-in-community. It is in and through community, or communities, that we grow up; community shapes who we are and who we become. In a radically relational understanding of the human the importance of community for the process of becoming who we are as human beings is highlighted, and the existence of communities that value openness, inclusivity, diversity and equality is assumed. Such communities foster relationships of mutuality, reciprocity and unity – not to be confused with uniformity. Most of all, such communities recognise that the human person as radically relational exists only as embodied, not therefore as disembodied spirit or soul. Embodiment is a key element in determining who we are, since it is through embodiment that we relate and communicate and discover our personal and distinctive identity.

A further feature of being constituted as relational persons is our inescapable awareness of belonging to the wider community of creation. Here it must be emphasised that we are part of nature, not outside nature, or above nature, but in nature. Humans are not separate from nature and its ecological processes. On the contrary, we depend on nature and its complex processes in so many different ways: air, soil, water, food, light, darkness, rivers, rocks, trees ... We are not external observers but rather participants in the drama of life that belongs to the natural world, the community of human beings and the wider world of creation.

It should be noted that it is not only human beings who are constituted by relationships. Science suggests that all entities in the natural world are constituted by different and varying degrees of relationality. For example, atoms, cells, molecules, eco-systems, the solar system and the universe are all configured by a vast network of complex relationships. These relationships arise out of a dynamic movement from simplicity to complexity, from intense interactions to the emergence of something that is different and new. The new is not just a putting-together of parts, but the appearance of something different that cannot be reduced to a collection of previous parts.[20] The new emerges out of concentrated interactions between different entities at a lower level, rising to a configuration of new entities at a higher, more complex level. These developments are uneven and unpredictable. They do, however, point towards the presence of an underlying relationality that permeates the whole universe. Humans are constituted by relationships, the natural world is also constituted by different degrees of relationships, and the mystery of God as Trinity is constituted by divine persons. The relationality of human beings represents a particular intensification, crystallisation and complexification of what is taking place in the natural world. This emphasis on relationality, on inter-personal relationality, cannot be reduced to rules or calculations or objective facts as some would have us believe. Instead, we are dealing with something deeper that goes beyond empirical calculation or control.

There are different dimensions to the dynamics of inter-personal relationships and inter-subjective communication. These dimensions include: mutual trust and participation; a recognition of the presence of vulnerability within relationships; the necessary exercise of agency within human relationships; and the primacy of love. The importance of these elements can only be sketched here.

At the centre of most relationships is the presence of trust. The existence of trust is a presupposition in every relationship. Without trust the dynamic between two human beings changes into something else, such as control and exploitation, or utilisation and objectification of the other. Without trust good relations cannot come to life. Following close on trust comes the importance of participation. Participation involves a shift from being an observer to personal engagement, from being outside the relationship to being a participant within the relationship. The view from the inside of a relationship gives us what Paul Tillich describes as 'participative knowledge'. From participation we move into the area of vulnerability. A theology of relationality that does not take account of the existence of human vulnerability within relationships runs the risk of being an empty rhetoric or some kind of romantic delusion. Every relationship has an enduring element of vulnerability, which is precisely the reason why relationships require enduring commitment if they are to grow. Vulnerability entails exposure to success or failure, disappointment or enhancement, suffering or flourishing. Within the toing and froing of a relationship there is the opening up of oneself to the other. This process of opening up can change us for the better, and even bring about transformation; in some instances, it can change us for the worse, and have a negative impact. Relationships are fragile, containing the possibility of enhancement or diminishment, at one and the same time.

This fragile and vulnerable character of human relationships begs the question: What is it that sustains relationships, that keeps relationships in existence? The initial response to this question is the exercise of agency, which is key to maintaining relationships in existence. Without concrete actions and experiences of trust, the relationship will falter. However, the more foundational answer to this question of sustaining relationships is the existence of the primacy of love within the conduct of relationships. It is above all else the action of love that ignites a living relationship. It is the experience of loving and being loved that activates something deep within the interior of the life of another human being. It is the gift of love that awakens the innate capacity within every human being to love. The giving of love activates the return of love. It is at this level of love, and the primacy of love, that the movement from anthropology to theological anthropology takes place.

At the core of Christianity, there is a teaching about the primacy of love, summed up in the great commandment to love God and neighbour. According to the Christian commandment, it is not that we first decide to love God, and then God loves us. Rather, it is the opposite, namely that God first loved us and it is that gift of God's love that enables us to love God and our neighbour. That God first loved us is not immediately self-evident in life, instead it is in the experience of being loved by the other that the love of God for us is revealed more often than not. Through the experience of love, we are able to discover the presence of the love of God as given, as something already there, in the love of one human being for another. It would be incorrect to hold that this is the only way that the love of God is revealed. There are other ways in which the love of God is revealed. It could be the experience of the absence of love in our lives that reveals the presence of the love of God, or the love of God can be revealed in and through the gift and abundance of God's creation, especially in and through the beauty of creation. Equally, it could be through the experience of suffering, or a sense of being abandoned that the love of God can break through. There are many surprising ways in which the love of God breaks into life, to sustain and enrich and deepen the love of one human being for another. At the centre of these many manifestations of the love of God is the particular revelation of the love of God in the life, death and resurrection of Christ, who discloses and embodies the love of God made flesh. The two main theologians of the New Testament, Paul and John, give us some sense of the priority of the love of God in life. It is in Paul's First Letter to Corinthians (15:1–13) that a full account of love is given:

> If I speak in the tongues of mortals and of angels, but have not love, I am a noisy gong or a clanging cymbal … if I have all faith, so as to move mountains, but do not have love, I am nothing. If I give away all my possessions, but do not have love, I gain nothing.

And then Paul puts before his audience the following challenge of love:

> Love is patient ... kind ... not envious or boastful or arrogant or rude ... does not rejoice in wrongdoing, but rejoices in the truth. It bears all things, believes all things, hopes all things, endures all things. Love never ends ... And now faith, hope, and love abide, these three; and the greatest of these is love.

It is perhaps John who gives the fullest theology of human love and divine love. He begins by encouraging us to 'love one another' (1 John 4:7), because 'love is from God'. John goes on to point out that 'everyone who loves is born of God and knows God'. Then comes the strong statement that 'whoever does not love does not know God', and the reason for this is that, for Christians, 'God is love', and that love of God has been revealed to the world in the sending of his son into the world so that we might live through him. And then comes a key Christian insight about love and the human capacity for love:

> In this is love, not that we loved God but that he loved us and sent his son among us.

If it is love that activates relationships, and if it is the love of God that sustains them, that says something vitally important about the Christian God, namely that not only is the human made in the image of God but, more importantly, that the human is made in the image of love in virtue of the Christian definition of God as love. The human carries in her being the imprint of love and this hallmark of love is stamped on the being of every person. Love is not just another dimension of the human; love is at the core of human identity and human flourishing because we are made in the image of a God who is love.

Closely connected to this emphasis on the centrality of love to anthropology is a more careful look at what was happening in the historical life, death and resurrection of Jesus. There is a dimension to the life of Jesus that tells us something about what it means to be a human being. He lives a life of service, dedicated to the coming reign of

God. It is also a life driven by love and a particular understanding of love which is summed up in the Parable of the Seed:

> I tell you, unless the grain of wheat dies, it remains just a single grain; but if it dies, it bears much fruit. (John 12:24)

Jesus offers a brief explanation of this parable in the following way:

> Those who love their life, lose it, and those who hate their life in this world will keep it for eternal life. (John 12:25)

There is a dynamic here that entails a letting-go of the self to find oneself, a process that is sometimes described in terms of self-emptying, which gives rise to self-discovery. This is known as *kenosis*, a letting-go of the self to find oneself in the other, a process of self-surrender to discover something deeper about oneself. The exemplar of this is found in the self-emptying of Jesus on the cross into God. This self-emptying leads to the fullness of life (*plerosis*) which is called resurrection. In other words, there is a unity between death and resurrection, between self-surrender and self-discovery, revealed in the death and resurrection of Jesus on the cross, often referred to as the Paschal Mystery of Christ, that is a passing over from the old to the new, from a self-centred life to a life centred on another. This is telling us something fundamental about what is involved in being human. It was this insight, among others, that prompted the Second Vatican Council to say 'it is only in the mystery of the Word made flesh that the mystery of humanity truly becomes clear ... Christ ... fully reveals humanity to itself and brings to light its very high calling'.[21] The dynamic of the Paschal Mystery reveals a pattern of self-emptying leading to self-discovery, of dying to the old and rising to the new. This process contains a profound insight into what it means to be human. A sense of that meaning is captured in another statement at the council which suggests that humans 'can fully discover their true selves only in sincere self-giving'.[22] A fuller expansion of this understanding of what is involved in being human is found in *Laudato Si'*:

> The human person grows more, matures more, is sanctified

more, to the extent that he or she enters into relationships, going out from themselves to live in communion with God, others and with all creatures. (*LS*, 240)

This model of *kenosis*, of dying to self to find oneself, is open to misunderstanding and abuse according to some feminist thinkers, especially when practised by those who are already oppressed. In these circumstances, self-emptying can become an experience of further oppression, instead of being an experience of empowerment and liberation. Therefore, it must be pointed out that the anthropological model of self-emptying is not meant to be a negation of the self; rather, it is intended to be an experience of newfound freedom and emancipation.[23] From this brief account of a self-emptying model of anthropology, we can move to some Trinitarian dimensions of what it means to be human.

There is a further dimension to this Christian teaching about God who is love, and that is the revelation of the life of this God as Father, Son and Spirit in history. And here we are moving from the Christological foundations of anthropology to a Trinitarian understanding of anthropology. Without adopting a social Trinitarianism, we can say, none the less, that the doctrine of the Trinity reveals a radically relational anthropology. Not only are human beings made in the image of God who is love, they are also made in the image of God, whose definition requires references to the interior and exterior relationality of Father, Son and Holy Spirit. This statement is based on the relationship of the Father and the Son in terms of the Father's love for the Son (the *abba* experience) with the Spirit as the bond of unity within that love. Put into a more contemporary idiom, we can say that the Trinity personifies the transformation of the 'twosomeness' of the Father and the Son in the 'threesomeness' of Spirit, Son and Father.[24] This threesomeness of the Trinity is glimpsed in the love of one human being for another, in which there is the presence of the love of God.

Broadly speaking, the doctrine of the Trinity down through the ages has gravitated back and forth between the western tradition, which emphasises the unity of God, and the eastern tradition, which has focused on the existence of three divine persons within God. The challenge of any Trinitarian doctrine of God is to keep these two contradictory dimensions on the Christian God together. What this life of love within God in history tells us, according to Catherine LaCugna, is this:

> The ultimate source of all reality is not a 'by itself' or an 'in itself' but a person, a toward-another.[25]

It is this outward looking reality, this outgoing self-communication of God, that is inscribed into the heart of all beings, and into the core of the human condition, created as they are by a Trinitarian God and, therefore, bearing the image of this dynamic, perichoretic Trinitarian God.

Further, all reality, because it comes from a Trinitarian God, is radically relational. This does not mean the being of God, the ultimate reality of God, precedes relationality:

> It is not the case that something first is what it is, and then that it enters various relationships; rather being and relationship are simultaneous.[26]

What this means in effect is that the persons of the Trinity are not just relations, but rather that the three divine persons are persons in relation to each other. As Aquinas puts it, divine persons are 'subsistent relations', that is, persons subsisting only in relation to each other.

As Declan Marmion and Rik Van Nieuwenhove remind us, this understanding of person and relation 'as used in reference to the Trinity can only be applied to the human community in an *analogous* rather than a univocal way'[27] – a timely reminder concerning all statements about God which contain an important element of *docta ignorantia*, as seen in Chapter 1.

One further point about this condensed account of the inter-relational character of the Trinity is that it could be said to be reflected in the scientific understanding of the world as deeply interconnected.[28] At the very least it can be said that such an understanding of the Trinitarian God as inter-relational does not explicitly conflict with, or overtly contradict, contemporary science in its understanding of physical reality as deeply relational and dynamic.

In brief, I am arguing in the first instance for a new frame of reference. It goes beyond the transcendent frame that imagines external forces shape the world presented in the 'Big History'. It also goes beyond the immanent frame that excludes from its imagination any depth in either the cosmic or the anthropological that could reveal the love of God. This frame is a relational frame and provides the context for working out a Trinitarian theology of human identity. Neither extrinsic supernaturalism nor reductionist naturalism can fully understand the world in which we live. This world, if we learn how to see it right, can shown us the divine in and through creation and every part of it. We shall return to this question in Chapter 4, which seeks to relocate the human within the larger community of creation and not outside creation.

CHAPTER 3

Integral Ecology and Deep Pneumatology

THERE HAS been a notable neglect of the spirit in Western theology. There are reasons for this neglect. These include: the existence of an excessive Christo-monism, a narrow concentration on grace, the mechanisation of nature and the consequent disenchantment of the universe caused by modern science, the exploitation of the natural world as a raw resource for use by human beings without regard to the interiority and integrity of the life of nature, the confinement of the spirit to institutionalised Christianity and the emergence of what is called a 'nature deficit disorder' in the lives of many caused by urbanisation. There are, of course, exceptions to this generalisation, such as Jürgen Moltmann, Yves Congar, Elizabeth A. Johnson, Denis Edwards and Amos Yong. It is often remarked that if we took the spirit seriously, we would have different theologies of the Church and of creation today.

The Neglect of Pneumatology
This neglect of the spirit in the natural world has shut the door on an important source for understanding the spirit of God in the book of nature. This marginalisation of the spirit within contemporary culture is so striking that the Canadian philosopher, Charles Taylor, has suggested that it is as if modern man had suffered from what he calls 'a spiritual lobotomy'.[1] Others point to the presence of spirit-stifling practices that have become embedded in modern culture: the pervasive presence

of market-driven capitalism, endless distractions caused by modern technology and the contagion of consumerism. A further impediment to engagement with the spirit is the presence of damaging dualisms: body and soul, sacred and secular, matter and spirit.

It is against this background that we hear calls for a recovery of what some refer to as 'a nature-based Pneumatology',[2] and others describe as a theology of nature as spirit-graced to its core.[3] Echoes of this need for a new theology of the spirit can be found in statements like 'I'm spiritual but not religious'. This observation is, of course, highly ambiguous and can signify different things. For some, it is a desire to deliberately distance themselves from institutionalised Christianity. In the US in the last ten years, the third largest religious grouping was that of ex-Catholics who cited the absence of a meaningful spirituality as their main reason for leaving the Church. This absence of a meaningful spirituality may have shifted in the light of more recent revelations in relation to sexual abuse in the Catholic Church. For others, this statement about being spiritual but not religious can be a *cri de coeur* for something to fill the gap left by organised religion. Here, however, we want to reflect the concerns of another group that desires some kind of alternative, non-institutionalised spirituality, and even the possibility of a theology of the spirit. Alongside this phenomenon it should be noted there is some evidence of a new spiritual awakening taking place among young and old who have become disaffected from all institutions, whether religious, political or economic. It is not just a coincidence that Pope Francis, in *Laudato Si'*, talks about the need for 'an ecological spirituality'.[4] There is a growing awareness that the ecological crisis is fundamentally a spiritual crisis.

In response to this neglect of the spirit and the emerging search for some kind of spirituality, it is not enough to trot out the hard-won, classical theology of the spirit summed up in the Nicene-Constantinople Creed in response to calls for a new pneumatology. The Nicene Creed affirmed belief in the Holy Spirit as 'the Lord and Giver of life', as equal to the Father and the Son, and therefore as worthy of worship alongside the Father and the Son. Without wishing to diminish the importance of this conciliar teaching, it is now necessary to go back behind the Nicene Creed to its basis in the New Testament, and behind the New

Testament to its foundation in the Hebrew scriptures and behind the Jewish theology of the spirit to its roots in primordial experiences of nature and history.

In the Christian imagination, a theology of the spirit is too often seen as something that began with Pentecost, fifty days after the Easter event. If that were the case, it would mean that, somehow or other, the life of Jesus and the existence of Judaism were spirit-less. For too many and for too long, pneumatology has been seen as a Christian reality. However, Jewish scholar John R. Levison, correctly in my opinion, points out that 'Christian Pneumatology becomes less about an exclusively Christian experience or doctrine, and more about the presence of God in the grand scheme of *Israel's* history – and Christianity as ancient Israel's heir.' For Levison, the 'essence of Christian Pneumatology, therefore, should be traced deep into the heart of the Hebrew scriptures.'[5] Those very scriptures point us to the natural world.

What is needed at this time is a renewed theology of the spirit which at the same time recognises that the ecological crisis is a deeply spiritual crisis. There is also a growing awareness that this renewed theology of the spirit should begin with what commentators call 'a pneumatology from below'.[6]

One can only agree with Levison in stressing the importance of going back to the Jewish roots of Christian pneumatology. However, to grasp the richness of the Jewish theology of the spirit, it is necessary to go back to its foundation in primordial experiences of the spirit, not only in history, but also in the encounter of the spirit in nature. At the same time, it must be stated that there is something distinctive about the Christian experience of the spirit: it is Messianic, it is about an encounter with the distinctive spirit of the risen Christ, and it is sacramental.

What is involved in the adoption of 'a pneumatology from below'? It is an encounter of the spirit rooted in human experience, in the experience of nature, in the experience of other human beings, and in the experience of charismatic figures in history. A 'pneumatology from below' seeks to find a foothold in the many interpretations of what is going on in the crucible of human experience. A 'pneumatology from below' will learn some lessons from the adoption of a 'Christology from below', which that took place in the last century in the writings of Paul

Tillich, Wolfhart Pannenburg, Edward Schillebeeckx and Karl Rahner. This move in the last century gave rise to a renaissance in Christological studies. If half the number of books written on Jesus in the twentieth century could be written on the experience of the spirit with the same critical and historical rigour, then the landscape of religion and particularly of Christianity would be different today.

It should be emphasised that 'pneumatology from below' seeks to complement, critically and constructively, the classical 'pneumatology from above', as worked out at Nicaea/Constantinople. Another way of viewing a 'pneumatology from below' would be as a low-ascending theology of the spirit. At the same time, it must be acknowledged that a 'pneumatology from below' will contain an element of a 'pneumatology from above', because the experience of the spirit is ultimately an experience of something already given as gift.

In emphasising the importance of the experience of the spirit, we should be aware that references to the experience of the spirit are fraught with ambiguity and open to many misunderstandings. To take account of this ambiguity, it may be helpful to outline what an experience of the spirit is *not*. Karl Rahner, who explicitly affirms the possibility of an experience of the spirit, sought to highlight what is distinctive in this experience. He pointed out that the experience of the spirit is not of the same order or on the same level as the experience of objects in the world. An experience of the spirit is not an encounter with an object alongside other objects, nor is it an item of information alongside other items of information, nor is it an explanation alongside other explanations. Further, it should be noted that the experience is not to be found in the normal course of events as some kind of external or supernatural intervention in the natural processes of biological evolution and human development. The spirit is already present and active in these natural processes of evolution; it is 'we' who are absent or inattentive to this ongoing presence of the spirit. In other words, the spirit 'breathes where it will' in many surprising ways: in the life of nature, in the movements of history, in prophets and holy persons, in holy things, in cultures and religions, in the creative arts and the insights of modern science, in the awakening of human consciousness and the discovery of human interiority. An experience of the spirit is more about the spirit finding us than about us creating the spirit. In other words, an experience of the spirit is not a human projection but a discovery of what is already there in the world, not a merely human construction but the active unravelling of a gift already given, not a projection but a making explicit of that with which we are already familiar. When we ignore the presence of the spirit, we do what T.S. Eliot warned of:

> We had the experience
> But missed the meaning.[7]

This means the experience of the spirit is not some kind of exotic, sensational encounter with a disembodied entity. Instead, the experience of God is often the experience of the most ordinary things of life which, through attention and focus, can take on extraordinary, even mystical signification.

Universal Experiences of the Spirit

In the light of these qualifications of what might count as an experience of the spirit, we need to look at some broad experiences as well as specific experiences of what might count as an experience of the spirit. In general terms, we will look briefly at three broad experiences of the spirit: in the experience of nature, in the encounter of another human being and in the reality of human consciousness.

From time to time, we encounter a vital life-force in nature that is initially just a matter of fact and then, suddenly, assumes a deeper significance, striking a chord within the interior recesses of our being. This experience of nature can of course be positive or negative, since we know that nature can be both uplifting as well as crushing. Such an experience might be an encounter with stars on a moonless night, or the discovery of the hidden life of trees through their outward appearance. One expression of this experience of nature can be found in a poem entitled 'Postscript', by the Irish recipient of the 1995 Nobel Prize for Literature, Seamus Heaney (1939–2013). It is worth quoting in full:

> And some time make the time to drive out west
> Into County Clare, along the Flaggy Shore,
> In September or October, when the wind
> And the light are working off each other

So that the ocean on one side is wild
With foam and glitter, and inland among stones
The surface of a slate-grey lake is lit
By the earthed lightening of a flock of swans,
Their feathers roughed and ruffling, white on white,
Their fully-grown headstrong-looking heads
Tucked or cresting or busy underwater.
Useless to think you'll park or capture it
More thoroughly. You are neither here nor there,
A hurry through which known and strange things pass
As big soft buffetings come at the car sideways
And catch the heart off guard and blow it open.[8] (Italics added)

Heaney's own commentary on this poem is instructive. He describes this experience as 'a side-long glimpse of something flying past; before I knew where I was, I went after it'. This experience, he says, leaves one 'with a sensation of having been visited'.[9] Catching 'the heart off guard' and 'blowing it open' captures for many what an experience of nature can do from time to time. For those unfamiliar with what is known as the Wild Atlantic Way in the west of Ireland, a similar experience can be found in the US, in Muir Woods, north San Francisco. In 2018, I visited the woods and observed a family entering that part of the woods known as 'The Cathedral Grove'. A ten-year old child, struck by the beauty, elegance and majesty of the redwood trees, whispered to his parents: 'Shhh, you are not supposed to speak in here!'

Another similar but different expression of the link between nature and the spiritual network of eternal life can be found in Heaney's poem 'St Kevin and the Blackbird':

And then there was St Kevin and the blackbird.
The saint is kneeling, arms stretched out, inside
His cell, but the cell is narrow, so

One turned-up palm is out the window, stiff
As a crossbeam, when a blackbird lands
And lays in it and settles down to nest.

Kevin feels the warm eggs, the small breast, the tucked
Neat head and claws and, *finding himself linked*
Into the network of eternal life,

Is moved to pity: now he must hold his hand
Like a branch out in the sun and rain for weeks
Until the young are hatched and fledged and flown.[10]
(Italics added)

The experience of being 'off guard' and having one's heart 'blown open' can also happen in the encounter with another human being and in the gift of friendship. This happens when the other awakens the dormant inner self of another human being, and suddenly the 'I' of the observer is captivated by a 'thou' of the other. Our lack-lustre selves are unexpectedly energised and empowered by the experience of the other. It is this encounter with the human spirit of another that puts us in touch with something deeply spiritual in the other or, indeed, in ourselves. Often, it is the human spirit that mediates the invisible Holy Spirit.

A third broad experience that can put us in touch with the experience of the Spirit of God is the discovery of human consciousness, especially reflective self-consciousness. Human consciousness is a distinctive feature of what it means to be a human being. The philosopher, John Eccles, sums up this uniqueness of the human in the following way:

Let us be clear that for each of us, the primary reality is our consciousness – everything else is derivative and has a second order reality.[11]

Reflective self-consciousness is a given, a primal reality that evolves and deepens over time. It is the place where we discover the spiritual depths of our humanity and realise that we are not just a biological mass. Human consciousness connects us to other human beings and invites us to reach out beyond ourselves in a movement of self-transcendence. It is within this movement of self-transcendence that we experience the desire, the unrestricted desire, to know and to love and to ask endless questions, especially why there is anything rather than nothing. This drive of reflective self-consciousness to know and to love and to question can awaken an experience of the spirit of God as already given.

The rise of interest in human consciousness is alive and well in contemporary culture: in courses on mindfulness, in meditation and in the quest for well-being, each of which is an expression of the search for some kind of spirituality, or at least an openness to a quest for some form of life in the spirit. The quality and depth of consciousness expands over time, when we ask searching questions about origins: the origins of the cosmos, of biological evolution and the emergence of the human within the vast history of fourteen billion years. An awareness that the development of human consciousness is the outcome of an expanding cosmology and ongoing biological evolution leaves the human wondering and searching for new, deeper spiritual possibilities. Moments within this expanding consciousness can be signalled symbolically in this diagram:

Big Bang
Energy
Particles
Atoms
Matter
Stars
Molecules
Earth
Biological life
Human life
Consciousness
Self-consciousness
Reflective self-consciousness
Spiritual consciousness
Historical consciousness
Global consciousness
Human interiority
Freedom and responsibility
Care and compassion
Solidarity
A universal communion within diversity

We can now move from these three generic experiences of the spirit in nature, in other human beings and in the given-ness of consciousness, to an outline of some specific instances of these experiences. Here we will focus on three examples: the experience of the *indwelling* spirit, the *renewing* spirit and the *inspiring* spirit.[12]

Specific Experiences of the Spirit

When we look at the earth, at the interior life of nature, at the uniqueness of the individual, we sense an indwelling presence of a life-giving force that animates the earth, the life of nature and the uniqueness of the human. This life-giving force is immanent in varying degrees throughout the world; it is found as omnipresent in the earth, in nature and in each other.

It is perhaps the nature poets who capture most effectively this 'indwelling-presence of the spirit' in the world. Gerard Manley Hopkins (1844–1889) observes:

> The world is charged with the grandeur of God.
> It will flame out, like shining from shook foil;
> It gathers to a greatness, like the ooze of oil
> Crushed. Why do men then now not reck his rod?
> Generations have trod, have trod, have trod;
> And all is seared with trade; bleared, smeared with toil; ...
> And for all this nature is never spent;
> There lives the dearest, freshness deep down things; ...
> Because the Holy Ghost over the bent
> World broods with warm breast and with ah! bright wings.[13]

A similar sense of the indwelling of this life-giving energy can also be found in Wordsworth who tells us how, in his mature years, he had been able to sense in nature

> A presence that disturbs me with joy
> Of elevated thoughts; a sense sublime
> Of something far more deeply interfused
> Whose dwelling is the light of setting suns,

And the round ocean and the living air,
And the blue sky, and in the mind of man;
A motion and a spirit that impels
All living things, all objects of all thought, and rolls to all
things.[14]

The psalmist echoes this omnipresence of the spirit in the following way:

> Where can I go from your spirit
> Or where can I flee from your presence.
> If I ascend to heaven you are there
> If I make my bed in sheol you are there
> If I take the wings of mourning and settle at the furthest limit
> of the sea
> Even there your hand shall lead me
> And your right hand shall hold me fast. (Psalm 139:7–10)

And then the same psalmist, moving on in continuity from the earth to the human, affirms

> For it was you who formed my inward parts;
> You knit me together in my mother's womb'.
> (Psalm 139:13–14)

This gift of the spirit is experienced and understood to be indwelling throughout the universe. Of course, this presence of the spirit is beyond the purview of scientific materialism. It cannot be empirically observed, but this is hardly an argument against the possible experience of this presence of the spirit.

This sense of the indwelling spirit stands out in sharp contrast to the disenchantment of the universe wrought by modern science. The adoption of an integral ecology as a response to the environmental crisis opens the way for a recovery, as seen in Chapter 1, of the interiority of all living things and, therefore, as a new space for the possible experience of the spirit.

Alongside the indwelling spirit in the world, we can discern the existence of 'a renewing spirit' throughout the life of nature. There is present in nature a spirit that continuously rejuvenates the earth through the seasons of the year and the reproductive cycles of nature. This process of the ongoing renewal taking place in nature is often taken for granted. However, when renewal is interfered with, or interrupted, as is happening with climate change and the loss of bio-diversity, we begin to see the gifting character of renewal in a new light. On the one hand, we appreciate the gift of renewal and, on the other hand, we are challenged to safeguard the integrity of this gift of renewal and to ask the question: what is it that powers and energises such renewal? This renewing experience is captured by the Belgian poet, Catherine de Vinck (1922–), who on the one hand notes how time seems simply to go on and on and:

> Yet the gifting never ceases:
> Nests fill with eggs, fields swell
> With edible plants,
> Water continues to rise out of deep, hidden wells
> Pulled by the moon, sea waves unscroll themselves
> Foaming on the beach.
> What disappears returns
> Defying decay and death. In a corner of the yard
> A single tulip blooms year after year
> Naming itself red and new
> In the spring air.[15]

Again, it is the psalmist who senses this ongoing renewal in the following way:

> You caused the grass to grow for the cattle
> And plants for people to use
> To bring forth food from the earth. (Psalm 104:14)

And then he goes on to note that:

When you hide your face, they are dismayed;
When you take away their breath, they die and return
    to their dust
When you send forth your spirit they are created;
And you renew the face of the ground. (Psalm 104:29–30)

The third specific experience of God is that of the presence of *an inspiring spirit*. What is it that draws the best out of people, that energises them to make a difference, that drives them to go the second mile, that animates them to go on mission to the ends of the earth? Who or 'what is it', to borrow the words of Stephen Hawking, that 'breathes fire into equations and makes a universe for them to describe'?[16] It is this fire, this energy, that inspires the creativity that takes place in the arts, in the humanities, in the breakthroughs of scientists in laboratories, and that inspires the lofty thoughts of the religions of the world. The prophet Isaiah senses this inspiration as that which takes place throughout the earth and, in particular, in generation after generation:

For I will pour out water on the thirsty land
And streams on dry ground.
I will pour my spirit upon your descendants
And my blessings on your offspring.
They shall spring up like a green tamarisk [a shrub or a small
    tree]
Like willows by flowing streams. (Isaiah 44:3–4)

It is this inspiring spirit that is the source of creativity and drives so much novelty and innovation in the world. The image invoked to capture this action of the spirit in the world is that of 'midwife'.[17] As midwife, the spirit is present throughout the processes of giving birth: inspiring, enabling and facilitating new life in the world around us. Another image often invoked to describe the action of the spirit is that of a 'mother hen hovering' over the surface of the waters in the opening verses of Genesis 1. Others talk of the spirit as a 'bird brooding' over the universe, seeing the spirit as one who presides over the affairs of the world, bringing light out of darkness, the new out of the old, and life out of death.[18]

The Spirit in the Hebrew Bible

These primordial experiences of the spirit, both broad and specific, suggest that a closer look at what the Hebrew bible has to say about the spirit may be enlightening. One of the most commonly used terms in the Jewish Bible is the Hebrew word *ruach*/spirit. This term is found in 378 places, far more than the word 'covenant' (289), or 'mercy' (251) or 'peace' (237).[19] It is impossible to capture the uniqueness of Judaism without reference to this Hebrew word *ruach*. It has many shades of meaning which are difficult to grasp without reference to their context.

For some, *ruach* means spirit, wind or breath.[20] For others, such as Theodore Hiebert, *ruach* has many meanings: atmosphere, breath, God's atmosphere, God's breath, the first sacred thing, and the breath of all creatures.[21] Hiebert prefers to use the word 'breath' in order to avoid some of the ambiguity attaching to spirit.

Probably the oldest account of the spirit is found in the Yahwist story of creation in Genesis 2 – a text that goes back to somewhere between the tenth and ninth century BCE. In verse 7 it is stated:

> … then the Lord God formed man from the dust of the ground, and breathed into his nostrils the breath of life; and man became a living being. (Genesis 2:7)

Alongside this text there is the influential priestly account of creation in Genesis 1:1–2:

> In the beginning when God created heaven and earth,
> The earth was formless and darkness covered the face of the deep,
> While a wind from God swept over the face of the waters.

This text is notoriously difficult to translate. Interpreters are divided on the appropriate translation of the word '*ruach*'. Most English translations (NRSV and NABRE and the New Jewish Publication Society) render *ruach* as wind. It is pointed out that the wind here may just be part of the 'formless void' and 'darkness' that preceded the act of creation and, therefore, should not necessarily be thought of as the wind or breath of

God. It is further noted that the act of creation is the result primarily of the creative Word (of God) and, therefore, we should not read too much into the use of the word *ruach* in this context. On the other hand, there are some, especially among Pentecostal theologians, who argue that the presence of the spirit of God is the presupposition of the utterance of the Word of God.[22] In support of this particular interpretation they point to Psalm 33:6, which is explicit about the joint activity of the spirit and the Word in the act of creation:

> By the *word of the Lord* the heavens were made,
> And all their host by the *breath* of his mouth. (Italics added)

Clearly there is room for some debate here and therefore the opening verses of the priestly account of creation in Genesis 1 can hardly be taken on their own as a foundation for developing a Hebrew theology of the spirit. There are other texts that should be invoked in any discussion about the role of the spirit in creation. These include the Psalms, the Book of Job and the prophet Ezekiel.

Psalm 104 reflects on the universal presence of the spirit in the world. This psalm emphasises experiences of air, water, fire and earth, which are found in many religions and, at the same time, this psalm refers also to the role of the spirit in sustaining these primordial experiences of life.

Psalm 104 begins:

> Bless the Lord, oh my soul (1)
> You ride on the wings of wind (3)
> You make wind your messenger, and fire and flame your ministers (4)
> You set the earth on its foundations so that it shall never be shaken (5)
> You make the springs gush forth in the valleys (10)
> From your lofty abode you water the mountains (13)
> You ... bring forth food from the earth. (14)

Then, the author of this psalm goes on to associate these basic experiences of air, water, fire and earth with the activity of the spirit:

When you hide your face, they are dismayed
When you take away their breath they die and return to their dust.
When you send forth your spirit they are created;
And you renew the face of the ground. (Psalm 104:29–30)

This perspective on the spirit is echoed in other places in the Hebrew Bible. For example, Job, in his dialogue with God, points out:

In his hand is the life of every living thing and the breath of every human being. (Job 12:10)

And further:

As long as my breath is in me, and the spirit of God is in my nostrils, my lips will not speak falsehood and my tongue will not utter deceit. (Job 27:3)

Continuing this theme, Job says:

The spirit of God has made me
And the breath of the Almighty gives me life. (Job 33:4)

And then, finally:

'If he (Elihu) should take back his spirit to himself
And gather to himself his breath,
All flesh would perish together
And all mortals return to the dust. (Job 34:14–15)

Another significant text that uses the word *ruach* with slightly different meanings is the dry bones prophecy of Ezekiel 37:1–14. This text opens:

The hand of the Lord came upon me and he brought me out by the spirit (*ruach*) of the Lord and set me down in the middle of the valley.

The text closes:

> I will put my spirit (*ruach*) within you and you shall live.

The use of *ruach* as divine spirit at the beginning and at the end is consistent. Thereafter, however, it is best translated as 'breath':

> Thus says the Lord to these bones:
> I will cause breath to enter and you shall live (5)
> I will put my breath in you and you shall live (6)
> I looked, and there were sinews on them, and flesh had come
> upon them ... but there was no breath (*ruach*) in them. (8)
> Then he said to me prophesy to the breath (*ruach*), prophesy
> mortal, and say to the breath (*ruach*): ... o breathe, breathe
> (*ruach*) upon these slain that they may live. (9)
> I prophesied ... and breath (*ruach*) came into them.

The use of *ruach* as breath in these verses shows how flexible the term *ruach* is and how necessary it is to go beyond a single or a simple translation of *ruach* as spirit.

Taken together, this limited selection of texts, and many others not mentioned here, add up to a rich, nuanced and differentiated range of meaning attached to the Hebrew word *ruach*. That range of meaning includes at least the following points:

- What makes a human alive is their participation in the divine *ruach*. (Genesis 2: 7; Ezekiel 37: 1 and 14; and Isaiah 42: 5)
- The *ruach* of God is involved, not only in the lives of humans, but also in the lives of other creatures and the life of the earth. (Psalm 33: 6)
- The gift of life in humans, in other creatures, and in the earth comes from the *ruach* of God and depends on the *ruach* of God. (Psalm 104:27–30)
- The *ruach* of God is not only the source of life, but it is also an active force in life enabling humans to carry out

divine tasks. (Numbers 24:2, 11:25 and 29; Micah 3:8)

- The *ruach* of God comes across as an active energy empowering the life of nature to be both productive and reproductive. (Isaiah 44:3–4)
- There appears to be a close relationship between the human spirit and the Holy Spirit. (Psalm 33:6; 104:29–30)

What is striking about this Hebrew theology of the spirit is that the spirit is earthy: dwelling in dust, in nostrils, in bodies and in the material elements of air, water, fire and earth. Some commentators talk about the 'earth-loving spirit'[23] and others refer to 'a faith that loves the earth'.[24] It should be emphasised that the mindset of the biblical authors in their treatment of the presence of *ruach* does not allow a division, or separation, or split between body and soul, the human and the non-human, nature and spirit. Such dualisms are unbiblical, unfaithful to the text and foreign to the vision of the Jewish scriptures.[25] It is this underlying unity between spirit and matter that is an outstanding part of the Hebrew theology of the spirit and, as such, has a certain resonance with the principle of materiality running through contemporary cosmology, biological evolution and human emergence. As Roger Haight observes, there is: 'a material consistency through the galaxies to our solar system and right down to each single person', and this in turn 'gives the reality of the universe a steady commonality and inter-relatedness; everything comes from the same material elements, atoms and sub-atomic particles'.[26]

Teilhard on the Unity of Spirit and Matter

One scientist who was fascinated by matter throughout his life was Teilhard de Chardin (1881–1955). In 1919, de Chardin wrote an article on 'The Spiritual Power of Matter', which concluded with a well-known twenty-verse 'Hymn to Matter'.[27] A sample of what he wrote in the 'Hymn to Matter' includes:

> Blessed be you, harsh matter, barren soil, stubborn rock …
> Without you … we should remain all our lives on earth,
> Ignorant both of ourselves and of God.

He then goes on to say:

> I acclaim you (that is matter) as the divine milieu, charged
> with creative power as the ocean stirred by the Spirit, as the
> clay moulded and infused by the Incarnate Word.[28]

Matter, for Teilhard, was the place where the divine resides. Looking
back over his life, Teilhard saw that his love of matter enabled him to
say that 'matter is the matrix of the Spirit' and that 'Spirit is the higher
state of matter'.[29]

Spirit and matter are not separate entities that are loosely joined.
Instead, they are intimately connected dimensions of one and the same
entity. For Teilhard, matter is imbued with a spiritual component. This
enabled him to recognise the incarnate presence of the Spirit in the
world and this helped him to overcome the separation of matter and
spirit.[30]

Teilhard's understanding of matter was developed and refined further
in 1936 when he wrote:

> All that exists that is matter becoming.
>
> There is neither spirit nor matter in the world; (instead) the
> stuff of the universe is spirit-matter.
>
> No other substance but this could produce the human
> molecule.[31]

Later Teilhard suggests that 'the time has come for us to realise that
to be satisfactory, any interpretation of the universe … must cover the
inside as well as the outside of things – the spirit as well as matter'.[32] This
prescient remark is echoed today among many philosophers, scientists
and theologians who acknowledge the interiority of matter alongside
its exteriority. The advances of science in the last fifty years, especially
in developing new, powerful microscopes and nano-technology, has
enabled scientists to see a new world in a way never before possible,
disclosing a fascinating inside world of matter. This new technology

reveals something of the micro-architecture of the inside of matter, compared by some to the mind-blowing inside of a beehive.[33] In a different context, Cambridge theologian Janet M. Soskice notes: 'that matter as congested energy is just as much a mystery as anything one might call spirit'.[34]

This emphasis by Teilhard on the unity of spirit and matter is taken up and developed by Karl Rahner. For Rahner, there are three fundamental reasons why Christian faith must affirm this unity of spirit and matter, namely the doctrine of creation, the historical evolution of the world under the influence of the spirit, and the destiny of spirit and matter in terms of the new creation inaugurated by the death and resurrection of Christ. In discussing the unity of spirit and matter, Rahner seeks to overcome the negative perception of matter as dark and anti-divine, obscure or chaotic. Rahner sees matter as endowed from the beginning with a dynamism towards spirit. He describes this orientation in terms of the self-transcendence of matter. The emergence of the human spirit in evolution is, in a manner of speaking, the fulfilment of matter.[35] This fulfilment of matter in the advent of the human is matter 'becoming conscious of itself'.[36] The human is the cosmos becoming conscious of itself.[37] In the light of evolution, we can say that matter becomes life and life becomes conscious of itself in the human and that the future of the human has been prefigured in the bodily resurrection of Christ from the dead.[38] In the light of this understanding of the unity of spirit and matter, Rahner suggests that 'we Christians … are the most sublime materialists because we cannot see the fullness of reality without thinking also of matter as enduring in a state of perfection'.[39] To justify these theological statements, Rahner goes on to say that the inner dynamic of matter 'is the *Holy Pneuma* of God'.[40]

This science-sensitive thinking of Teilhard and Rahner, and the theological perspectives it opens up, are not alien to the Christian tradition. Part of that tradition sees a close relationship between the Creator and creation in the early Christian doctrine of creation out of nothing (*creatio ex nihilo*). Further, classical theology has insisted on the unity of the immanence and transcendence of God in the world, the unity of nature and grace, and the unity of creation and salvation. This underlying unity is grounded in the outpouring of the spirit on all flesh from the dawn of time and the Christian doctrines of the bodily resurrection of Christ and the making flesh of the Word in Jesus, doctrines that will be taken up in Chapter 4.

Examples of this close relationship between God and matter can be found in John Damascene (675–753) who, in his defence of icons, wrote:

> I do not worship matter. I worship the God of matter, who became matter for my sake and deigned to inhabit matter, who worked out my salvation through matter. I will not cease from honouring that matter which works for my salvation.[41]

In the Middle Ages, Bonaventure saw matter as spiritualised, seeking perfection.[42] Though Bonaventure knew nothing of evolution, he saw matter as dynamic, with an underlying orientation towards a higher form, namely the human condition. Through the human, matter seeks union with God, which happens through the agency of the spirit in the world and the Incarnation of the Word of God in Jesus. For Bonaventure, matter is loaded with spiritual possibilities, and these possibilities derive from the action of the spirit in creation. A prototype of this involvement of God in creation is given in the Incarnation.[43]

Echoes of the above emphasis on the presence of the spirit throughout the universe can be found in different places in *Laudato Si'*:

> The spirit, infinite bond of love, is intimately present at the very heart of the universe, inspiring and bringing new pathways. (*LS*, 238)

> The spirit of God has filled the universe with possibilities and, therefore, from the very heart of things, something new can always emerge. (*LS*, 80 and 88)

At the same time, there are also echoes in *Laudato Si'* of the theological significance of matter as outlined above:

> … the life of the spirit is not dissociated from the body or

from nature or from worldly realities, but lived in and with them, in communion with all that surrounds us. (*LS*, 216)

Equally significant is where *Laudato Si'* says:

The entire material universe speaks of God's love, his boundless affection for us. Soil, water, mountains: everything is, as it were, a caress of God. (*LS*, 84)

To gather up these fragments into some kind of unified perspective we can say it is the spirit, the Holy Spirit of God

- who spins the globe;
- who powered the unfolding of the cosmos 14 billion years ago;
- who enabled the evolution of biological life some 4.5 billion years ago;
- who inspires the unique emergence of human beings some 200,000 years ago.

It is the same Spirit

- who midwifes the new in human affairs, in the arts and in the sciences;
- who raises up the broken and the bruised;
- who holds together in a creative unity the opposites of life and death, light and darkness, suffering and transformation.

In effect, symbolically speaking, and in varying degrees, the Spirit sleeps in stones, dreams in flowers and dances in human beings.

In other words, this initial, primordial pneumatology seeks

- to provide a foundation for a new dialogue between ecology and theology;
- to awaken motivation for the initiation of a new,

transformative ecological *praxis*;

- to offer a point of entry for those who self-describe as 'spiritual but not religious' for engagement in building bridges between human beings and the natural world;
- to suggest a basis for engagement in the much-needed dialogue between faith and science, spirit and creation;
- to open up a complementary relationship between the descending order of Spirit, Son and Father and the ascending order of Father, Son and Spirit.

This recognition of the presence of the Spirit in nature provides a new frame for some intractable theological problems. For example, the dichotomy between the explanation of salvation as freely given and salvation is shown to be false. In the twentieth century, Catholic and ecumenical theology have been much more explicit in recognising that salvation is first and foremost a gift of God and only secondly, if at all, a human achievement. Our position goes beyond that. In every moment of our lives, the Spirit is present in power. The question is whether we recognise and respond to the Spirit in what we do. We can ignore the Spirit. Indeed, our technological culture may well encourage or distract us to do so. But if we recognise the Spirit and heed the Spirit's calling to us to see and to reflect beauty, unceasingly uncover the truth, and respond to all there is gratefully and graciously, we are indeed saved.[44]

By way of conclusion, it must be said that this chapter on the possibility of developing a deep pneumatology is quite incomplete. It lacks reference to the importance of Christology for understanding pneumatology. It neglects the relationship that exists between the inhabitation of the spirit in creation and the Incarnation of the Word in all flesh – which are not in competition with each other but are, rather, Trinitarian actions of the one God. It also omits to outline criteria for discerning the presence and action of the Spirit in the world. Some of these questions and others will be taken up in Chapter 4.

CHAPTER 4

Deep Ecology and Deep Christology

THE ADOPTION of an integral ecology as outlined in Chapter 1 demands a mutually critical interaction between ecology and Christology. The emergence of what some call a deep ecology opens up new challenges and opportunities for the development of a deep Christology as articulated by the Danish theologian, Niels Henrik Gregersen, in terms of deep Incarnation.[1] This chapter will look at what contribution Christology can offer to the current ecological emergency and, at the same time, examine what deep ecology has to say to Christology.

We begin with a number of ecological questions for Christology. Why is there such a separation between the natural world and Christology? What does Christology have to offer to an ecological understanding of nature? Where does Christology fit in with the new cosmic story? What does Jesus have to say about the earth? Concerning this last question, care must be taken to avoid giving the impression that twenty-first-century questions about ecology can be answered by the early Church's understanding of the Christ-event. It is, however, possible that Christology can offer a new vision and new perspectives, and open up wider horizons in support of ecological issues.

Alongside these questions from ecology to Christology, there are also questions from Christology to ecology. Can an integral ecology help Christology to better understand the organic unity of all things in Christ? Is it possible that deep ecology can open up a new pathway for the incorporation of the natural world into Christology? How might deep ecology pave the way for a much-needed recovery of the cosmic Christ?

These questions pose a series of new internal challenges and opportunities for Christology in the twenty-first century. These challenges include the following foundational issues for the conduct of Christology in the light of the ecological emergency:

- The need to overcome the separation of creation and Christology.
- The importance of invoking the teaching of Chalcedon in a way that embraces the unity between Jesus as a child of the cosmos and the Word made flesh as complementary.
- The necessity to outline a unified Scotist view of salvation as an alternative to the dualistic understanding of salvation as separate from creation.
- A retrieval of Jesus as the Wisdom of God incarnate.

It is interesting to note how Rahner had highlighted a variation of these questions before the advent of the ecological crisis. Throughout his life, Rahner was keenly aware of the need to unify the relationship between creation and Incarnation. He sought to present creation and Incarnation as one divine action 'with two moments within the one process of God's self-communication to the world, although it is an intrinsically differentiated process'.[2] Towards the end of his life, Rahner highlighted the need for Christology 'to find an intelligible and orthodox connection between Jesus of Nazareth and the cosmic Christ, the omega point of world evolution'.[3] How is it possible to establish an underlying unity between the Jesus of history and the cosmic Christ of faith which, at the same time, acknowledges the transformation that takes place within this unity? In the last century much time was given to the quest for the historical Jesus. The focus has now shifted to the quest for the cosmic Christ as important for the critical interaction between ecology and Christology.

The Presence of Wisdom, Word and Spirit in the Hebrew Bible

In the first instance, we can only begin to address these questions and challenges by adopting a low-ascending Christology, that is, a

Christology that attends first to the experience people had with the cross of Jesus, in contrast to an approach that starts from the teaching of the Council of Chalcedon in 451 CE.[4] Further, in beginning with Jesus of Nazareth, we must locate him within his own context of Judaism. The Jewishness of Jesus is all-important in understanding the theological significance of the Christ-event. An important part of the Jewishness of Jesus is the various elements that make up the faith of Jesus. These include the foundational presence of an Exodus-faith in the life of Jesus. This Exodus-faith celebrates the liberation of the people of Israel from slavery in Egypt. This historical liberation was led by Moses in the thirteenth century BCE and gave rise to a legal agreement drawn up at Sinai, described as a Covenant between Yahweh and the people of Israel. This foundational moment is sometimes referred to as Exodus-1 because it was followed by a new Exodus or a second Exodus, when the people of Israel returned to Jerusalem from their captivity in Babylon in the sixth century BCE. At the time of Jesus, some Jews expected another Exodus-event and, for Christians, this came with the death and resurrection of Jesus, sometimes referred to as Exodus-3.[5]

A second key element within the faith of Jesus would have been the presence of a strong creation-faith. This creation-faith of Jesus, as indeed the Exodus-faith of Jesus, would have been formed by different, but complementary, experiences of God, experienced as encounters with the Wisdom of God, the Spirit of God and the Word of God. These aspects are central to Israel's faith-understanding and Jesus' faith understanding of creation and Exodus, and therefore the faith understanding of Jesus' disciples today. A brief, schematic summary of Wisdom, of Spirit and of Word is essential background to the development of Christologies in the New Testament.[6]

The figure of Wisdom is prominent in the Hebrew Bible. There are six books describing her activities: Job, Proverbs, Ecclesiastes, the Song of Songs, Sirach and Wisdom. Wisdom, in the Book of Proverbs, is personified and portrayed as representing the feminine face of God: 'Before the beginning of the earth, I [Wisdom] was brought forth, when there were no springs' (Proverbs 8:23–24). And 'when he established the heavens, I was there' (Proverbs 8:27). Equally important is the Book of Wisdom, which describes Wisdom as 'more beautiful than the sun' and the One who 'excels every constellation of the stars' (Wisdom 7:29).

The Spirit (breath) of God is a key presence throughout the Hebrew Bible. The Spirit of God is described as the creative source of life (Genesis 1 and 2; Psalm 104:29–30), the one who inspires and guides prophets (Isaiah 61:1–2; Ezekiel 3:12, 8:3, 11:1) and the one who renews the face of the earth (Psalms 33:6 and 104:29–30). At times, the Spirit is closely connected to the figure of Wisdom, so much so that some books talk about 'the spirit of Wisdom' (Wisdom 7:7; Deuteronomy 34:9).

And, thirdly, there is a strong presence of Word, of the Word of God, throughout Judaism. The Word of God is creative, as in Genesis 1 and Psalm 33:6, and is personified in the Book of Wisdom (Wisdom 18:14–16) and embodied in the utterances of the prophets who hear the Word (Jeremiah 1:2; Ezekiel 1:3). Further, the Word is a guide and a light (Psalm 119:147), the source of life and healing (Deuteronomy 8:3), the one 'who is very near to you' and is 'in your mouth … and in your heart' (Deuteronomy 30:14).

These perspectives on Wisdom, Spirit and Word are different, but complementary, expressions of the presence of the one and the same God. Each represents activities of God in creation, in history, in the lives of leaders and prophets. What is striking about these actions of God is the equivalency, parallelisms and intimate relatedness between all three, though perhaps this is not so surprising because they derive from a strict monotheism that is the hallmark of Judaism, in contrast to its neighbours. It would be misleading to give the impression that there was a worked-out, systematic theology of Wisdom, Spirit and Word in the Hebrew scriptures. It would be more accurate to suggest that there is a scattered, but consistent, presence of Wisdom, Spirit and Word at work in the lives of the people of Israel. This is a presence seeking further clarification and completion. It is the formal claim of the New Testament that this completion takes place in the life, death and resurrection of Jesus. Without reference to this Jewish background of Wisdom, Spirit and Word, as expressions of the Exodus-faith and creation-faith, it would be impossible to make sense of the New Testament and the plurality of Christologies it presents.

A Plurality of Christologies in the New Testament

We will begin with Wisdom Christology because it is the earliest Christology of the New Testament. It was the Wisdom traditions that served in the first instance as the 'generative matrix' of early Christology.[7] Further, according to J. D. G. Dunn, it was Wisdom Christology that paved the way for the doctrine of the Incarnation.[8] In addition, according to Raymond Brown, in his commentary on the Gospel of John, Jesus is 'the culmination of a tradition that runs through the Wisdom literature of the Old Testament'.[9] Much of the language and theology of the Hebrew Bible on Wisdom resonates within the Gospel of John and is explicitly applied to Jesus. Raymond Brown finds at least twelve clear parallels between Jewish Wisdom and the teaching of John on Jesus.[10] This discussion will be limited to four explicit parallels between the *Logos* prologue of John's Gospel and the figure of Wisdom in the Hebrew Bible.

Firstly, Wisdom existed with God from the beginning (Proverbs 8:22–23), just as the *Logos* existed in the beginning (John 1:1). Secondly, Wisdom is said to be a pure emanation of the glory of the Almighty (Proverbs 17:5) and the *Logos* in John reflects the glory of God (John 1:14). Thirdly, Wisdom is said to be a reflection of the everlasting light of God (Wisdom 7:26), whereas in John's Gospel, the light of the *Logos* is the light of world (John 1:4–5). Fourthly, Wisdom is described as having descended from heaven to dwell with the people (Proverbs 8:31; Sirach 24:8), whereas in John the *Logos* descended from heaven to earth (John 1:14).

According to Elizabeth Johnson, behind every line about the Word/ *Logos*, there lies a story of Wisdom; she adds: 'The Prologue, we might say, transposes into the key of *Logos* the music that was originally written in the key of *Sophia*.'[11]

This same language is also present to a lesser degree but no less real in the Synoptics. For example, in Luke's Gospel, Jesus says that 'Wisdom is vindicated by all her children' (Luke 7:35), whereas in Matthew, Jesus says that 'Wisdom is vindicated by her deeds' (Matthew 11:19). There is a shift taking place here from Jesus as a child of Wisdom to being Wisdom in person. In brief, it is possible to discern a gradual development in the four Gospels from Jesus as a teacher of Wisdom to being a child of Wisdom, to being Wisdom in person, to being Wisdom Incarnate.

In addition to the Gospels, reference must also be made to the explicit Wisdom-Christologies in Paul and the Deutero-Pauline Letters. We will confine ourselves here to just two examples. In Paul's Letter to the Corinthians, in answer to the question 'Where is the one who is wise?', Paul affirms that 'God has made foolish the Wisdom of the world', and then goes on to affirm that:

> We proclaim Christ crucified, a stumbling block to Jews and foolishness to Gentiles. But to those who are called, both Jews and Greeks, Christ the power of God and the Wisdom of God. (1 Corinthians 1:23–24)

At the end of that Chapter, Paul goes on to say that God who 'is the source of your life in Christ Jesus … became for us Wisdom from God' (1 Corinthians 1:30).

In 1 Corinthians 2, Paul also points out that 'we do speak Wisdom, though it is not a Wisdom of this age' (1 Corinthians 2:6). 'Instead we speak God's Wisdom, secret and hidden, which God decreed before the ages for our glory' (1 Corinthians 2:7).

A second example of Wisdom Christology can be found in Colossians 1:15–20, which presents Christ as:

> The first-born of all creation;
> for in him all things in heaven and in earth
> were created …
> All things have been created through him and for him.
> He himself is before all things and in him all things hold together …
> He … is the beginning, the first born
> from the dead.

Whenever Christ is given a role in creation, or is present at the beginning of all things, the intention is that Christ is taking on a role that was previously given to the figure of Wisdom in the Sapiential literature. This theme of Christ as the Wisdom of God is continued in Ephesians 1:3–10, Philippians 2:5–11, Hebrews 1:2–3 and the Prologue of John's Gospel.

In conclusion to this brief overview of Wisdom Christology, it must be pointed out that the word 'Wisdom' is feminine, as used in the Hebrew Bible and now applied to Jesus. Sophia, in the Sapiential literature, expresses features of what we see as 'feminine' in the mystery of the one God, features that have been forgotten and neglected within the largely Patriarchal reception of the Jewish and Christian scriptures. If Christology is to be inclusive as originally intended, and if the strong emphasis in Paul and John on the unity, equality, and dignity of all 'in Christ' and 'in the Spirit' is recognised, and if the patristic principle of what is not assumed is not redeemed is accepted, and if the carefully chosen language of Chalcedon, which talks about *homo* and not *vir*, is respected, then the patriarchal bias of traditional Christology will have to be critiqued Christologically and Pneumatologically, especially in the light of the centrality of the Wisdom Christology of early Christianity.

There are good theological reasons why Wisdom Christology should be given greater emphasis at this time:

- It connects Christology with the theme of creation which is so prominent in the Sapiential literature of the Bible.
- It serves as a bridge in the dialogue between ecology and Christology.
- It retrieves the impulse towards a radical inclusivity that was part of the earliest understanding of the Christ-event (for example Galatians 3:28; Romans 16:1–27).
- It recognises aspects of the Christ-event, often thought of as feminine, that are part of the Gospel of Christ.
- It contributes important dimensions to the twenty-first-century quest for the Cosmic Christ.
- It captures the transformation of Patriarchy that is important for the renewal of ecology and ecclesiology.
- It overcomes the perceived tension between historical Christology and cosmic Christology.

Closely linked to the centrality of Wisdom Christology in the New Testament is the presence of a Spirit-Christology. Given the connection seen between Wisdom and Spirit in the Hebrew Bible, one would expect some similarity as well as difference between Spirit-Christology and Wisdom-Christology.

As seen in Chapter 3, *Ruach* is prominent in the Hebrew Bible. Most significantly, the Spirit in Judaism is an 'earth-loving-spirit',[12] dwelling in dust, nostrils and the matter of creation. Similarly, the activity of the Spirit in the New Testament is bound up with bodies. For example, Luke, who has most to say about Spirit in the infancy narratives and in the Acts of the Apostles, outlines what the angel says to Mary:

> The Holy Spirit will come upon you, and the power of the most high will overshadow you; therefore the child to be born will be holy. (Luke 1: 35)

The Greek word used for the overshadowing of Mary, *epeskioso,* is the same word used in the Septuagint for the action of the Spirit over the primeval waters in Genesis 1:2. Clearly, Luke intends to establish a link between the first creation in Genesis and the new creation which is about to take place in the Christ-event. For Luke, Elizabeth and Zachariah and John the Baptist are 'filled with Holy Spirit' (Luke 1:41 and 67), and the Holy Spirit we are told 'rested' on and 'guided' Simeon (Luke 2:27). The public ministry of Jesus begins with the descent of the Spirit at his baptism by John the Baptist. In Luke, 'Jesus, full of the Holy Spirit, returned from the Jordan and was led by the Spirit into the wilderness' (Luke 4:1). After forty days in the desert, Jesus returned to Galilee 'filled with the Holy Spirit', entered the synagogue on the Sabbath and opened the scroll where it says:

> The Spirit of the Lord is upon me
> because he has anointed me to bring good news to the poor …
> to proclaim release to the captives
> … sight to the blind, to let the oppressed go free
> and proclaim the year of the Lord's favour. (Luke 4:16–19)

The public ministry of Jesus is animated by the Spirit and reaches a high point with the journey up to Jerusalem and the death of Jesus on the cross. Matthew's description and apocalyptic interpretation of this event is worth quoting in full.

> Then Jesus cried with a loud voice and breathed his last. At that moment the curtain of the temple was torn in two, from top to bottom. The earth shook, and rocks were split. Tombs were opened and many bodies of the saints who had fallen asleep were raised. (Matthew 27:50, 52)

Jesus breathing forth at his death echoes the Spirit of God breathing over the void and darkness in Genesis 1:2. Matthew's interpretation of this event, in terms of the earth shaking, rocks splitting and tombs opening, marks a transition from the Spirit active in the historical life of Jesus to the Spirit of Jesus now becoming active in the cosmos. This transition from the ministry of the historical Jesus to the beginnings of the cosmic Christ is recognised when Paul uses 'the Spirit of God' and 'the Spirit of Christ' interchangeably (Romans 8:9–11).

The third Christology in the New Testament that is of central importance for our purposes is the Word Christology/*Logos* Christology, summed up in the prologue of John's Gospel (1:1–14). The *Logos* Christology of John can be interpreted as a cosmic hymn in terms of the eternal Word of God entering into personal engagement with creation and then the history of humanity symbolised by 'flesh'. The *Logos* Christology of John has dominated the landscape from the second century onwards, especially on the rocky road from the Council of Nicaea (325) to Chalcedon (451). Some of the key verses in this fourteen-verse hymn are:

> In the beginning was the Word, and the Word was with God
> And the Word was God (1)
> He was in the beginning with God (2).
> All things came into being through Him,
> and without Him not one thing came into being.
> What has come into being in Him was life.

And the life was the light of all people.
The light shines in the darkness
and the darkness did not overcome it (5) ...
And the Word became flesh and lived among us,
and we have seen His glory.

Many background influences are at play in the composition of this unique Christological hymn: the Jewish theology of the Word, the centrality of Wisdom within Judaism, Hellenistic philosophy and its many variants. The hymn starts out 'In the beginning', clearly echoing 'In the beginning' in the opening verses of Genesis 1:1, and again in the second verse we are told 'he was in the beginning with God', which is an explicit reference to Wisdom who was present to God 'at the first, before the beginning' (Proverbs 22:22–31, at 22–23). This echo of Genesis continues in the prologue through the images of life, light and darkness (Genesis 1:4–5). This cosmic activity of the Word comes to a climax with the eternal Word descending into human history in verse 14: 'And the Word was made flesh and lived among us, we have seen His glory'.

These verses of John's prologue have been analysed through the centuries, and will continue to be exegeted until the Eschaton, because of the multi-layered complex history attached to the words *Logos* (Word) and *sarx* (flesh). It should be noted that the *Logos*/Word did not become a human being (*homo*) nor did the Word become a man (*vir*); instead, and far more radically, verse 14 claims that 'the *Logos* became *sarx*'. Everything hinges around the meaning of *Logos* and the multiple meanings attached to both *Logos* and *sarx*. We have already seen some of the meanings attached to the word *Logos* in the Hebrew Bible. The word flesh/*sarx* is wider and deeper than that of a human being (*anthropos*). From a biblical point of view, the flesh/*sarx* means at least the whole of the human being, and not just the soul or the spirit, but the whole corporeal reality of what is involved in being human: materiality, weakness, perishability, transience, vulnerability and mortality. The expression 'all flesh' appears in the Bible to remind us that the human belongs to all other human beings and the wider flesh-community of creation. There is a growing consensus that flesh means not only the full reality of a human being, but also includes at least the whole of biological creation in its beauty and brutality, as found with particular intensity in the life and death of every human being. This wider understanding of the meaning of the word 'flesh' has been facilitated by two related developments in the last fifty years.

From Deep Ecology to Deep Incarnation

In the early 1970s, Norwegian philosopher Arne Næss coined the expression 'deep ecology'. This term suggests that we need to go beyond a purely scientific approach to ecology. A deep ecology claims that non-human life forms have 'intrinsic value', and this value is 'independent of the usefulness these may have for narrow human purposes'.[13]

In 2001, Danish theologian Nils Henrik Gregersen adopted, with some reservations, Naess's deep ecology, moving the debate from a scientific-philosophical view of deep ecology to a theological consideration of deep Incarnation. Gregersen offers a number of descriptions of deep Incarnation. He sees it as the view:

- that 'God's own *Logos* (… Wisdom and Word) was made flesh in Jesus Christ … by assuming the particular life story of Jesus the Jew from Nazareth';
- that God 'also conjoined the material conditions of crea-turely existence (all flesh)';
- that God 'shared and ennobled the fate of all biological life forms ("grass" and "lilies") and experienced the pain of sensitive creatures ("sparrows" and "foxes") from within';
- that deep Incarnation is about 'a divine embodiment which reaches into the roots of material and biological existence as well as the darker sides of creation';[14]
- that 'the cross of Christ is here both the apex and the depth of Incarnation'.[15]

Gregersen's perspective will only make sense in the context of 'big history', as discussed earlier, namely the new cosmic story that traces the origins of the universe back some fourteen billion years to embrace an expanding cosmology, biological evolution and human emergence. Within this story, there is a line of continuity from matter to life and from life to mind, all of which are included in this new understanding of *sarx*. This particular perception of the world in which we live is accepted in broad outline by many commentators. In particular, the new cosmic story requires a reconfiguration of what it means to be human. However one might describe the human, it must include reference to a linkage between cosmology, evolution and human beings. This is part of the necessary backdrop for understanding the meaning of deep Incarnation. The flesh/*sarx* adopted by God in Jesus is part and parcel of the flesh/*sarx* that was born out of the expanding elements of the Big Bang story fourteen billion years ago and subsequent evolution. In this sense, Jesus of Nazareth is a child of the cosmos and so, when the Word/*Logos* was made flesh/*sarx*, the Word adopted the materiality of cosmic and biological evolution as well as the full reality of the human condition in Jesus. This activity of the Word did not begin with the Christ-event, but with the act of creation wherein the Word spoke: 'Let there be light … a dome … dry land … vegetation … lights in the dome … swarms of living creatures … great sea monsters and every living creature … human kind' (Genesis 1:3–28). Of course, these are not scientific statements in any sense; they are, rather, theological interpretations of the empirical data of the universe. The Word of God active 'in the beginning' in creation is continuously active in the world, in the history of Israel, and now in the Christ-event. The entry of the *Logos* into *sarx* in Jesus is not the first entry of the *Logos* into the world, but rather the completion of the continuous activity of the *Logos* in the world from the dawn of time. This important point is captured in Edward Schillebeeckx's perception of Christology as concentrated creation.[16] The Christ-event is a microcosm of what is continually taking place in the macrocosm of life and creation.[17]

Initial Evaluation of Gregersen's Deep Incarnation

It is time now to offer some evaluation of Gregersen's idea of deep Incarnation. Does deep Incarnation help to overcome the gap between creation and Christology? Will deep Incarnation reconnect Jesus with the natural world? Does it provide a way forward for the construction of a cosmic Christology?

Elizabeth Johnson points out that Gregersen's theology of deep Incarnation 'has set off a fruitful train of thought'.[18] At the same time, she signals 'several pitfalls that need to be avoided as this symbol continues to be developed'.[19] The first signal is that the Hellenistic view of the Word/*Logos* is centred around an orderly view of the world which ignores the disorder of random events that pervade the natural world. The presence of these disruptive events in the natural world appears to be an intrinsic part of evolution. Traces of such events can be found in the ministry of Jesus when he questions the prevailing order, and are most evident in *the* disruptive event of his own suffering and death on the cross of Calvary. On the other hand, it should be acknowledged that Gregersen is aware that the *Logos* of John's Gospel is not only the *Logos* of Hellenistic philosophy, but also the *Logos* of Jewish theology,[20] which is not the same. The second signal that Johnson issues is that the Word/*Logos* is masculine and is normally designated as 'He'. This gives the impression that when the Word became flesh, it became male, and this presents a male view of the incomprehensible mystery of God. However, as we have seen, the word *sarx* goes beyond male and female. The *Logos* of deep Incarnation, therefore, needs to be balanced by a Wisdom Christology and its representation of aspects that are often labelled feminine in the mystery of God. The third signal is that the dominance of the *Logos* Christology tends to drown out the equally important Spirit Christology. In this regard, Gregersen does say, in passing, that 'Deep Incarnation … involves a pneumatological perspective no less than a Christological view'.[21] However, this condensed pneumatological reference needs to be expanded.

Another participant in this debate about deep Incarnation is US philosopher Holmes Rolston III. He is concerned that the meaning of the word *sarx* in the prologue 'has been so stretched out that it begins to lose any specificity'.[22] Rolston questions the extension of the Incarnation to animals, plants, stones and all cosmic life systems. If the language of Incarnation is extended in this direction, then one must recognise and emphasise the symbolic character of this extension. Further, one must surely talk about differentiated degrees or modes of Incarnation. The Incarnation of the *Logos* in Jesus must be differentiated from the presence or, more accurately, the co-presence of the *Logos* in the history of Israel and throughout the community of creation. The universal presence of the *Logos* in creation is not the same as the Incarnation of the *Logos* in

Jesus. There is a difference between various incarnations of the *Logos* in creation, in the world of religions and in the history of Israel, and *the* Incarnation of God in the very particular person of Jesus of Nazareth. In distinguishing various modes of incarnation, care must be taken that one does not suppose that these different modes of incarnation are in any sense instances of *the* Incarnation

A further point about the possible loss of specificity, not mentioned by Rolston, is the possible neglect of what tradition calls 'the scandal of particularity'. Once again, in fairness to Gregersen, he anticipates this concern. He points, briefly, to a threefold expression of the scandal of particularity: the scandal of materiality, the scandal of suffering and the scandal of uniqueness.[23] What is at stake here is a very particular, historical specificity of the Incarnation: it took place at a very specific time in history, in a very particular place, and in very particular circumstances, namely the life and death of Jesus on the cross, captured starkly by Paul in 1 Corinthians when he states: 'We proclaim Christ crucified, a stumbling block to the Jews and foolishness to the Gentiles' (1 Corinthians 1:23). This historical particularity of the Incarnation does not rule out the universal significance of the Christ-event which is captured, not just in the *Logos* Christology of deep Incarnation, but also in the universal significance of Wisdom Christology and Spirit Christology. While the focus on Christ's particularity is crucial, it must avoid the pitfall of exclusivity. This is one of the contributions of deep Incarnation: it refuses to separate the Christ-event from any other event in creation. As noted in Chapter 2, everything is related. It is this relationship to the cosmos, the earth, society, religious traditions and other people that balances the potential pitfall of exclusivity.[24]

Deep Incarnation as presented by Gregersen is Christologically suggestive and timely in the light of the ecological emergency. It requires, however, further exploration, critique and refinement. It is not a Christology that can substitute for all other Christologies. It should be seen as belonging to the '*sic et non*' of Aquinas, or the famous '*placet iuxta modum*' of the Second Vatican Council. The real value of deep Incarnation is that it builds a bridge between Jesus and the natural world, and provides a basis for new dialogue between deep ecology and theology. Moreover, it opens the way for recovering the cosmic

Christ found in the Pauline literature of early Christological hymns, such as Colossians 1:15–20, 1 Corinthians 15:20–28, Ephesians 1:3–10 and Philippians 2:5–11. In doing just that, deep Incarnation enables Christology to transcend gender binaries. In addition, it confers a new dignity on the earth, recovers the intrinsic value of the earth's processes and life-systems and points to an underlying solidarity between the earth community and the human community. Lastly, deep Incarnation provides a supportive background for understanding Rahner's theology of the unity of creation and Incarnation.

The Underlying Unity of Creation and Incarnation

There have been two views on the relationship between creation and Incarnation. The more traditional view sees Incarnation as an 'add-on' to creation, a second act after creation. In this view, associated with Aquinas, God sent his son to remedy the arrival of sin through our first parents. The Incarnation, accordingly, appears as Plan B by virtue of the failure of Plan A in creation. In contrast to this outlook, there is the Franciscan view, found in Duns Scotus (1266–1308) and others, which sees the Incarnation as built into creation *ab initio*. This Scotist view has made a comeback in the light of our evolutionary understanding of the world. It was championed by Teilhard de Chardin and Karl Rahner in the twentieth century, and promoted by Elizabeth Johnson and Denis Edwards in recent times. At the risk of over-simplification, we can summarise the Scotist-Rahner views on the unity of creation and Incarnation in the following way. Incarnation is built into the interiority of creation from the dawn of time. The purpose of creation is to provide a suitable context for the advent of the Word/Wisdom/Spirit made flesh. Creation is about the outreach of God's self-communication in love to the world. This divine outreach in creation carries with it the gift of self-transcendence, bestowed on creation as the effect of God's outreach. Nature is graced from the beginning of time. There is a dynamic orientation within creation towards self-transcendence. This dynamic gift of self-transcendence is expressed in the evolution of the world: in the unfolding of cosmology, in the advent of biological evolution, in the emergence of the human and in the distinctive unity of God and *sarx* that took place in the Christ-event. There is an underlying unity, therefore, between creation and Incarnation. Creation is the expression of God's desire out of love to share God's self with the world. That self-communication of God in creation finds its fullest realisation in the life, death and resurrection of Jesus as Wisdom personally embodied in the flesh of Christ. Creation is oriented towards Incarnation, and Incarnation is the fulfilment of creation. Creation and Incarnation, therefore, are 'two moments and two phases within the one process of God's self- giving and self-expression, although it is an intrinsically differentiated process'.[25]

God implants, as it were, a dynamic orientation within creation through the gift of Word, Spirit and Wisdom. This orientation issues in the Incarnation of God in Jesus, and in the light of the Incarnation continues in the world towards its final consummation in Christ at the end of time. There are a number of advantages to this unified view of creation, Incarnation and consummation. The gift of self-transcendence, built into the orientation of matter in creation, and the dynamism of humanity provides a Christology that can engage with the science of evolution. This Christology is not an interventionist Christology but rather an unfolding Christology that resonates with the evolution of the cosmos as described by science. Further, the Christological unity of creation, Incarnation and consummation provides a perspective that can develop in constructive dialogue between deep ecology and deep Incarnation.

To conclude these sketchy reflections on deep Christology as found in the Incarnation of Wisdom, Spirit and Word in Jesus, we can sum up the overall direction of this chapter in a few sentences. Christology can be understood as 'concentrated creation'. Christology connects the macrocosm of the drama taking place in creation with the microcosm of that same drama in the life of Christ. Christology embodies the drama of life in its many and various expressions, but especially in the context of the ongoing presence of so much suffering and death in the world. Secondly, there is a need to give more attention to the prominence of Wisdom Christology in the New Testament. The development of Wisdom Christology is an urgent imperative for Christian faith in the twenty-first century, not only because of its cosmic orientation, but also because Wisdom Christology has the potential to open the way for the development of a fully-fledged feminist Christology, as a balance to the dominance, up to now, of male-centred Christologies. Thirdly, the time may be ripe to expand Congar's principle of 'No Christology without Pneumatology, and no Pneumatology without Christology' into 'no Christology without reference to Wisdom, Spirit and Word', and vice versa. In effect, it is essential that Wisdom Christology, *Logos* Christology and Spirit Christology mutually interact and correct each other in a way that is more faithful to the evidence of the Hebrew Bible and the New Testament.

CHAPTER 5

Eschatology and Ecology

ESCHATOLOGY IS an essential part of Christian theology. And yet, for various reasons, eschatology in the first half of the twentieth century had become isolated from the rest of theology. Karl Barth once described eschatology as a harmless tract coming at the end of theology, and J. B. Metz saw most eschatology as 'bland', lacking an 'apocalyptic sting'.[1] This sidelining of eschatology has left a hole in the rest of theology, bereft of essential elements such as the subversive and prophetic role of hope, the centrality of resurrection for Christian faith and the link between creation and eschatology. Basically, eschatology is about hope seeking experience, understanding and praxis in the company of faith and love. Hope is not the same as optimism. Optimism is an expectation of more of the same based on the law of human progress and development. In contrast, the logic of hope is based not on inference but on the logic of the imagination set on fire by the gift of the Spirit poured out on all of creation 'in the beginning'.

The term eschatology comes from the Greek word '*eschaton*', meaning the end time, or the last thing. The Bible has much to say about the end of time and the New Testament talks about the advent of the end of time in the person of Christ. Over time, eschatology was reduced to the study of the four last things (*eschata*), namely death, judgment, heaven and hell. This shift from the *eschaton* to the *eschata* gave rise to an understanding of eschatology as other-worldly, largely spiritual and futuristic in outlook with very little to say about life in this world, the importance of just social structures and the future of creation.

This other-worldly emphasis began to change in the middle of the twentieth century, with the renewal of biblical studies. It was noted, for example, that the eschatology of Jesus was both this-worldly and other-worldly, both social and spiritual, both historical and creation-centred. Further, the focus of Paul's letters and John's Gospel was seen as a reflection on the Christ-event as shaped by the advent of the *eschaton* in the life, death and resurrection of Jesus. The language of eschatology within the New Testament was about the arrival of the *eschaton* in Christ. Christ is portrayed as the first-born of all creation, the beginning of the end (Colossians 1:15–20), the first fruits of God's eschatological harvest (1 Corinthians 15:20–22). A key question in the early Church was: When would Christ return to complete what he had inaugurated in his life, death and resurrection? The relationship between the first coming of Christ and his second coming was much debated. Gradually, it dawned on the early Christians that the second coming of Christ, known as the *Parousia*, would not occur in their lifetime. This in turn issued in an emerging tension, a creative tension, between what had already been achieved in Christ and what was yet to come, a tension in Paul between 'the already' and 'the not-yet', between the realised eschatology of John and the futuristic eschatology of Paul.

In the light of the twentieth-century biblical renewal it has become clear that the key eschatological question is about the advent of the *eschaton* in Christ. What does it mean for us today to say that the end of the time has already taken place in the death and resurrection of Christ? How can we claim that the future has already arrived in Christ, that Christ prefigures the future of humanity, history and creation? How can we talk about the advent of the new creation in Christ? How do these central doctrines about Christ impact on the way we understand the present and the future? Clearly, the four *eschata* only make sense in the light of the advent of the *eschaton* in Christ.

It was in the context of this largely in-house debate in theology about eschatology that ecology arrived on the scene. Ecology brings a new set of questions for eschatology, and represents a new challenge as well as a new opportunity for eschatology. There are a number of important questions that ecology asks of eschatology. Living in this time, this apocalyptic time of climate emergency and the breakdown of bio-diversity, ecology asks eschatology to come down to earth. Is it possible for eschatology to apply the interest, energy and imagination devoted to other-worldly eschatologies through the construction of a this-worldly eschatology? What contribution could an immanent eschatology make to saving the planet from man-made destruction? Is it possible for eschatology to contribute positively to the struggle to protect the earth-based web of life, to safeguard the much-needed bio-diversity within nature, and to promote respect for the integrity of the earth? Can eschatology inspire and motivate ecological practices that will enhance the well-being of our common home? Can eschatology offer reasons for believing that planet earth has a future, or will the earth simply 'freeze or fry' at some time in the future, or will the inhabitants of Mother Earth simply destroy themselves through greed and over-consumption? One further question, among many other possible questions, is this: How can eschatology talk about the promise of a new creation in Christ when so much of the existing creation is in decline?

Theological Guidelines

To begin this conversation between ecology and eschatology, we need some basic theological guidelines. Eschatology will take a Christ-centred approach to these issues and seek to connect questions of ecology to the creation-based teaching of Jesus and the Paschal Mystery of his death and resurrection. This Christo-centric eschatology will, in turn, invoke a Spirit-based-understanding of creation and the advent of the new creation in Christ. This means working from a belief in the Creator-Spirit poured out at the dawn of time on the earth (*adamah*) and humanity (*adam*). The Spirit of God in Judaism pervades the whole of creation. The Spirit 'inhabits nature', 'rejuvenates' the earth and 'inspires' individuals. It is this Spirit, who continuously holds creation in existence, who will bring to completion the work of creation in the fullness of time. Further, an important link exists between creation and eschatology. This link is summed up succinctly by David Bentley Hart in the following way: 'In the end of all created things lies their beginning'. Hart continues: 'only from the perspective of the end can one know what all things are, why they have been made, and who the God is who has called them forth from nothingness'.[2] The end of things sheds light on their beginning.

A more contemporary approach to the relationship between beginnings and endings would be to start with creation and move from creation via Christology towards eschatology. The universe in the light of contemporary science is seen no longer as static but dynamic, no longer fixed but unfolding, no longer determined but emergent. We live in a world that is evolving, a world of possibilities and novelty and creativity. It is within this context of living in a world that is open-ended, processive and organic that new questions about eschatology arise: does the universe have a destiny or is it simply rudderless? Is the universe shaped by chaos or a combination of natural selection and randomness? Given the age of the universe (13.8 billion years) and its dramatic evolution over billions of years, it seems reasonable to hold that the universe as we know it is incomplete and unfinished, a work of art in progress. If this is the case, then the question of eschatology is inescapable.[3]

In other words, protology and eschatology are a single science, a single revelation disclosed in the God-man.[4] A close relationship exists between beginnings and endings, and between endings and beginnings. In this context, there is a need to overcome a confusion that often exists between the theology of creation and the scientific theory of cosmology. The doctrine of creation is not about a big-bang cosmology, nor is creation a scientific or explanatory belief about the beginning of the universe. It is important to acknowledge the boundaries that exist here between creation and cosmology as well as the affinities: one is theology and the other is science. In the light of these questions from ecology to eschatology, and the theological guidelines just outlined, we can now look at the relationship between creation and the new creation in Christ.

From Creation to the New Creation in Christ

There are a number of texts in the New Testament that deal with the future of creation, far too many to deal with here in any detail. These texts are pneumatological and Christological. Here we will look at some of the creation-centred Christologies. These different Christologies can be divided into four distinct, but related, categories: the new creation; the new heaven and the new earth; the Christological hymn of Colossians; and the groaning of creation in Romans 8.

The vision of the new creation in Christ appears explicitly in 2 Corinthians 5:17 and Galatians 6:15. How are we to understand the meaning of the new creation in these texts? It is revealing that the new creation in 2 Corinthians and Galatians was translated in the King James Version of the Bible as 'a new creature'. This gave the impression that the new creation in Christ was primarily anthropological, that is, human-centred. However, this interpretation changed in the twentieth century. The new creation is certainly anthropological, but it also includes the community of God's people (ecclesiology) and creation in a cosmological sense. This multi-layered meaning of the new creation is influenced in part by the presence of this theme in Isaiah (Isaiah 40:1–11; 43:11–21).[5] For Paul, the hope for a new creation will embrace individuals, the community of believers and creation. Within this biblical vision, all three are interconnected, and this vision is shaped by an inclusive theology of creation in Genesis, the Psalms, Job and Ezekiel.

The second category of New Testament texts is a theology of the new heaven and the new earth, which appears in the Book of Revelation 21:1–5, a text that echoes Isaiah 65:17, written during the time of the Babylonian exile:

> Then I saw a new heaven and a new earth; for the first heaven and the first earth had passed away … And I saw the holy city, the new Jerusalem, coming down out of heaven from God … 'see, the home of God is among mortals … see, I am making all things new. (Revelation 21:1–5)

Deutero-Isaiah, especially Isaiah 65:17–19, is part of the background. Equally significant is the appearance of a new heaven and a new earth in the last book of the Bible, coming as a completion of what began 'in the beginning' in the first book of the Bible. There is a relationship, as we have seen, between beginnings and endings, between Genesis and Revelation. This relationship between beginnings and endings is anthropological, communal and cosmological, a relationship of unity that reflects the holistic outlook of Judaism.

A second text referring to a new heaven and a new earth is to be found in 2 Peter 3:13:

> But, in accordance with his promise, we wait for the new heavens and the new earth where righteousness is at home.

This particular text is sometimes understood to mean the destruction of the present heavens and earth, and their replacement by a new creation. However, this interpretation goes against the integrated vision of Deutero-Isaiah in the Hebrew Bible and its realisation in the Christ-event as expressed in the bodily resurrection of Christ from the dead and the enfleshment of the Word in the Incarnation. The advent of the new heaven and the new earth is not about the replacement, but the renewal of creation, not about the destruction of the earth, but transformation, a point that will be taken up later in our discussion on the resurrection of Christ.

The third reference to the future of creation is the Christological hymn to the Colossians (Colossians 1:15–20). The context of this hymn, written around 60 CE, is a range of toxic teaching around syncretism, the cult of astrology and Gnosticism, each of which presented a challenge to the historical and cosmic significance of the Christ-event.[6] According to Paul:

1. The risen Christ *'is the image of the visible God'*. (15)
   The word 'image' echoes the Book of Genesis, which sees Adam and Eve as made 'in the image of God'(Genesis 1:27). The use of the image of the invisible God in Colossians is claiming that Christ has a special relationship with God, and this authorises him to represent God and act in his name.

2. The risen Christ *'is the first-born of creation'*. (15)
   The category 'first-born' is about the primacy of Christ, not just in relation to humanity, but also in relation to creation. Christ is at the centre of creation. There is a resonance here with the figure of Wisdom, who 'was set up at the first, before the beginning of creation' (Proverbs

8:22–23; Book of Wisdom 9:9). The risen Christ is perceived as the wisdom of God made manifest in history.

3. The risen Christ is the one in whom *'all things ... were created'*. (16)
   'All things' is intended to bring out the all-embracing significance of Christ. If there is any doubt about this inclusive significance of Christ, Paul goes on to spell it out in terms of things 'in heaven and on earth, things visible and invisible' (16). This inclusivity of the risen Christ is intended as a critique of the astral culture found in the territory of the Colossians.

4. *'All things have been created through him and for him'.* (16)
   This puts Christ at the beginning of creation, as well as making him the goal of creation, thus establishing the presence and the future of Christ as the beginning of creation and the end of creation.

5. The risen Christ *'is the beginning, the first-born from the dead, so that he might come to have first-place in everything'.* (18)
   This is the second time that Paul uses the language of the first-born. In the previous verse, Christ is the first-born of creation and now he is the first-born from the dead. This is a reference to the primacy of Christ's resurrection from the dead, and its significance for the followers of Christ. Once again, the primacy and centrality of Christ to the beginning and ending of creation is reiterated.

6. In Christ *'all the fullness of God was pleased to dwell, and through him God was pleased to reconcile to himself all things, whether on earth or in heaven'.* (19–20)
   This reference to the fullness of God dwelling in Christ is usually taken as a way of establishing the divinity of Christ. But, in the context of Colossians, it is more about

establishing the unique role of Christ as the representative or agent of God in a way that would have been impossible for the astral deities of the Colossian community. Instead, according to Paul, Christ is able to reconcile *all* things on earth and in heaven and this reconciliation takes place in history through Christ, and not in some ethereal or spiritual realm as some had been teaching the Colossians.

This Christological hymn captures the universal significance of the Christ-event: Christ affects humanity *and* the whole of creation, Christ is the first-born of all creation *and* the first-born from the dead, Christ is the beginning *and* the end of creation, Christ is the centre of creation who reconciles all things unto himself in heaven *and* on earth.

The fourth significant reference to creation in the New Testament is found in Romans 8, especially the creation hymn in verses 18–25. It will not be possible to do justice to this particularly rich theology of creation in this short space. A helpful analysis is provided by John Dillman in 'The Story of Creation, Believing Humanity, and God in Romans 8:18–25'.[7] Dillman outlines three story-lines or three acts within this narrative: creation, humanity and God. Concerning God, it would have been more helpful in his otherwise excellent analysis, to have spoken about not just God, but 'the Spirit of God', for reasons that will become apparent presently. Throughout this apocalyptic narrative there is an eschatological tension between suffering and glory (19), longing and revelation (19), futility and hope (20), slavery and freedom (21), groaning and redemption (23), seen and unseen (24–25), present and future (22).

Act I is about creation waiting with eager longing for the revealing of the children of God. In spite of being subjected to futility, creation hopes that it will be set free to obtain the freedom of the children of God (18–21). What is striking here is the personification of creation that awaits the unfolding drama of salvation. Further, there is a recognition that the future of creation is bound up with the destiny of humanity. In effect, there is an underlying unity between creation, humanity and the Spirit of God.

In Act II, the focus is on the believing community (22–25). This second act begins with the famous line that the whole of creation has been groaning in labour pains and not only creation but also humanity groans inwardly, awaiting the redemption of our bodies (22–23). Humanity and creation not only groan, but also hope as they wait in patience for what is not seen. For Paul, in this second act, what happens to humanity happens to creation.

Act III is about the activity of the Spirit within the unfolding drama of salvation. The Spirit is present and active throughout the story of creation and salvation. There are nineteen references to the Spirit throughout Romans 8. Immediately, following Act II, Paul tells us that the Spirit helps us in our weakness and in our solidarity with creation and humanity, and intercedes for us with sighs too deep for words. In this unique chapter of the Letter to the Romans, the Spirit is the One who, as agent:

- sets us free from the law of sin and death; (2)
- is the source of life and peace; (7)
- enables us to belong to Christ; (9)
- raised Christ from the dead and will give life to our mortal bodies; (11)
- puts to death the deeds of the body; (13)
- enables us to become children of God; (14)
- prompts us to cry '*Abba*, Father'; (15)
- inspires us to bear witness to being children of God and therefore heirs with Christ ;(16–17)
- helps us in our weakness; (26)
- intercedes for us. (27)[8]

This triple groaning of creation, humanity and now the Spirit highlights the solidarity between creation, humanity and the Spirit. Throughout the rest of Romans 8, the Spirit is active in many ways. In effect, it is the Spirit of God who is the agent of creation, of Christ's resurrection, the resurrection of humanity.

It should be noted that the three actors within this Hymn of Creation mutually illuminate each other. Each should be read in the light of the other. Separating them from each other runs the risk of distortion. Further, Paul teaches that creation has a future, and this future is bound up with the future of humanity. In addition, there is a profound unity between creation, humanity and the Spirit, symbolised in the triple groaning of creation, humanity and the Spirit.

Romans 8 presents a deeply Spirit-centred theology of the unfolding drama of eschatology. It would be tempting, but inaccurate, to say that Romans addresses the ecological challenges of the twenty-first century. Paul did not have the scientific understanding of creation or ecology available to us today. Yet it must be acknowledged that Romans 8 offers a vision, not an answer, that is pertinent to the ecological issues of today.

A further point is that Paul's personification of nature was particularly relevant to his readers in Rome. In Rome at that time there was a divinisation of nature that gave rise to the worship of nature-deities, and the ensuing presence of polytheism. The personification of creation by Paul parallels the Jewish personification of nature in many of the psalms (e.g. Psalms 19, 65, 96, 96 and 145). This personification of nature enabled Israel to safeguard its monotheism and, in the case of Paul, it implied a critique of the polytheism rampant in Rome at that time. It is hardly surprising that the Pauline scholar, Brendan Byrne, describes Romans 8 as 'one of the most singular and evocative texts of Paul'.[9]

From the Unified Biblical Vision to *Laudato Si'* via the Second Vatican Council

This New Testament vision of the new creation and the unity of all things in Christ is given expression in *Laudato Si'*. What is striking about that encyclical is the way it builds on the Bible and applies that unified vision to contemporary ecological concerns and challenges.

This move from the Bible to *Laudato Si'* is facilitated by developments that took place at the Second Vatican Council (1962–65) around hope and eschatology. Prior to the council, eschatology was individualistic, largely spiritual and other-worldly in terms of death, judgment, heaven and hell. At the council you had the beginnings of a move towards a this-worldly eschatology and a shift from the individual to the community and creation. The primary texts reflecting this shift are to be found in *Lumen Gentium* (The Dogmatic Constitution on the Church) (1964) and *Gaudium et Spes* (*The Pastoral Constitution on the Church in the Modern World*) (1965).

Lumen Gentium (*LG*) says:

> The Church ... will receive its perfection only in the glory of heaven, where the time for the renewal of all things will come' (Acts 3:21). At that time, together with the human race, the universe itself, which is closely related to humanity and which through it attains its destiny, will be perfectly established in Christ. (*LG*, 48)

Note the reference to the 'time for the renewal of all things' – not just individuals. Further, at that time, the human race and the universe, which is closely related to the human race and which through it attains its destiny, will be perfectly established in Christ. The eschatological vision of the Second Vatican Council is enlarged beyond the individual to include the communal and the universe, with the focus now primarily on Christ.

The Christological outlook is developed further in *Gaudium et Spes* in articles 38 and 39. Article 38 points out that, in the light of the resurrection, 'Christ is now at work in human hearts by the power of his Spirit'. Article 39 goes on to say that 'the form of this world ... is passing away', not the world, but the form of the world, and that God 'is preparing a new dwelling and a new earth'. It continues: 'Far from diminishing our concern to develop this earth, the expectation of a new earth should spur us on, for it is here the body of a new human family grows, foreshadowing in some way the age to come'. A link is established between this life and the life to come, and this paves the way for the development of a this-worldly and other-worldly eschatology. As if to drive home this point, it reaffirms the link between earthly responsibilities and spiritual responsibilities: 'It is a mistake to think that because we have here no lasting city ... we are entitled to evade our earthly responsibilities' (*GS*, 43). Most commentators point out, that in spite of the shift at the Second Vatican Council towards Christology, the recovery of the importance of the earth and the new emphasis on earthly responsibilities, the vision remains largely anthropocentric.[10] It is against the background of this progress at the Second Vatican Council that we can now turn to *Laudato Si'*.

There are shifts in *Laudato Si'*, far too many to summarise here. We will limit ourselves to the eschatological vision of humanity, the community of creation and the cosmos. Francis sees the book of nature as complementary to the book of the Bible and therefore as a source of Revelation (*LS*, 85). Nature is, as it were, an expression of 'God's art' (*LS*, 80). There is a plea throughout *Laudato Si'* to recover the dignity and the value of the natural world in itself (*LS*, 33), and not simply in its usefulness for human beings. He calls for a new relationship between humans and the natural world, and emphasises that 'God is intimately present to each being', that 'non-human creatures have a destiny appropriate to their condition', and that 'all creatures are moving forward, with us and through us, towards a common point of arrival which is God' (*LS*, 83). In the light of these broad theological shifts, which impact directly on ecology and eschatology, we will now summarise three significant moves in *Laudato Si'*.

The first move occurs in Section 83 which talks about 'the destiny of the universe', which 'has already been attained by the risen Christ'. In making this point, *Laudato Si'* gives a footnote to Teilhard de Chardin, which acknowledges 'the contribution Fr Teilhard de Chardin' has made.[11] Mention of Teilhard changes the eschatological register, transposing the reader into the mindset of a radical unity between spirit and matter, creation and Incarnation, within a universe moving towards Christ as the Omega point. Within this broad eschatological perspective, *Laudato Si'* deals explicitly with 'other creatures' who 'move forward with us and through us towards a common point of arrival'. Thus, 'other creatures' have a place in the *eschaton*; their purpose 'is not to be found in us' (*LS*, 83) since, as the encyclical says elsewhere, other creatures have a 'value in themselves' (*LS*, 33) and not in their usefulness to humankind.

The next move in *Laudato Si'* (*LS*,99) highlights the Christological foundations of eschatology: 'The destiny of all creation is bound up with the mystery of Christ, present from the beginning'. Here, references are made, in particular, to Colossians 1 and the prologue of John's Gospel. Through 'the Incarnation, the mystery of Christ is at work in a hidden manner in the natural world as a whole'. In paragraph 100, attention is drawn to another Christological foundation of eschatology, namely the resurrection. The risen Christ is 'present throughout creation by his universal Lordship', reconciling all things to himself, things in heaven and on earth. The same paragraph concludes by noting that 'the flowers of the field and the birds of the air' are now 'imbued with the radiant presence of the risen Christ'.

A third emphasis underpinning this eschatological vision is the presence of pneumatology. There are a few, but important, scattered references to the Spirit in *Laudato Si'* that are of key importance to eschatology. For example, paragraph 80 points out that 'the Spirit of God has filled the universe with possibilities and therefore from the very heart of things, something new can always emerge'. And again, the encyclical affirms that 'the Spirit of life dwells in every living creature and calls us to enter into relationship with him' (*LS*, 88). Towards the end of the encyclical, we are reminded that: 'the Spirit, infinite bond of love, is intimately present at the very heart of the universe, inspiring and bringing new pathways' (*LS*, 238).

There are at least two important doctrinal points in these particular references. On the one hand, the encyclical emphasises the indwelling presence of the Spirit in the universe from the dawn of time, that is the Spirit poured out on all creation, as expressed in the Genesis stories and repeated by Paul in Romans 5:5. On the other hand, the Spirit is the source of novelty, opening the way for new horizons and pathways. It is this indwelling presence of the Spirit that enables the new to appear in the creation of the world, in the history of Israel and in the advent of the new creation in Christ through his death and resurrection. And then, as if to drive home what the encyclical has been saying about the value of the natural world, it is stated that 'eternal life will be a shared experience of awe, in which each creature, resplendently transfigured, will take its rightful place' and have 'something to give to those poor men and women who will have been liberated once and for all' (*LS*, 243). This particular reference to other creatures being 'resplendently transfigured' is new in the teaching of the Church, and has been described by Nathan W. O'Halloran as 'a significant development of doctrine' building on the teaching of the Second Vatican Council.[12]

This new teaching of *Laudato Si'* is highly significant for the ecological movement. It highlights the value of non-human creatures and points to the responsibility of all to protect the integrity of the whole of creation: human beings, biological life, the interior life of the earth and the beauty of the cosmos. This unity of all things in Christ takes on new meaning because *Laudato Si'* makes it clear that 'all things' includes other creatures. If all things are destined to be part of a new creation in Christ, then all things must be respected for their value in themselves and not just for utilitarian reasons. As *Laudato Si'* says, 'the ultimate purpose of other creatures is not to be found in us' but in themselves as a valuable part of God's good creation. This new vision of *Laudato Si'* gives a new motivation for the safeguarding of bio-diversity, for the protection of oceanic life, for the reduction of man-made climate change, and for a new respect for the interior life of Mother Earth. In addition, this new vision opens up the way for developing more explicitly the importance of a this-worldly eschatology and its connection with ecology.

One other point that should be noted here in passing is the way the encyclical links eschatology with the celebration of the Eucharist: 'The Eucharist joins heaven and earth', and 'In the bread of the Eucharist, creation is projected towards divinisation' and 'towards unification with the creator himself' (*LS*, 236). This unique relationship between the Eucharist and eschatology will be developed in the final chapter of this book.

This grand eschatological vision of *Laudato Si'* builds on the eschatological vision of Isaiah which talks about the wolf living with the lamb, the leopard lying down with the kid, and the calf and the lion and the fatling living together (Isaiah 11:6). This vision of *Laudato Si'* requires further theological backing. What is it that enables and facilitates the realisation of this all-inclusive vision? There are at least two foundation stones for this perspective, one Christological and the other pneumatological. As already noted, these two perspectives must be kept together. Under Christology, reference has been made to the Incarnation and the resurrection. Under pneumatology the vision is first informed by, and dependent upon, the outpouring of the Spirit of God on all flesh and the deepening of that outpouring in the Christ-event, in what we have called Spirit Christology, and then by the 'Second Pentecostal' outpouring in the death and resurrection of Christ upon the disciples. Something needs to be said more explicitly about the key role of the resurrection of Christ in eschatology and for ecology.

The Pivotal Role of Resurrection in Eschatology

Discussions about the establishment of a new creation, the promise of a new heaven and a new earth, the presence of creation-centred Christological hymns in the New Testament, and the hope for the liberation of the groaning of creation are all premised on the reality of the resurrection of Jesus from the dead. As Paul puts it starkly:

> If Christ has not been raised, then our proclamation has been in vain and your faith has been in vain. (1 Corinthians 5:14)

There is a lot riding on the back of resurrection, yet the resurrection of Jesus from the dead is problematic for many modern people. The resurrection stretches human credulity from a philosophical and historical point of view; it seems to contradict the laws of nature. For some, the resurrection depends on some form of divine intervention from outside which goes against the grain of the new dialogue between religion and science. For others, the resurrection implies the reinstatement of belief in the discredited 'God of the gaps'.

To begin to address these difficulties, it may be helpful to clear up some misunderstandings around resurrection by saying what it is not:

- The resurrection of Jesus is not about the resuscitation or the revival of the physical body of Jesus as if to pick up seamlessly where he left off at death.
- The resurrection of Jesus is not about the immortality of the soul of Jesus.
- The resurrection is not a purely spiritual phenomenon, invented by the disciples of Jesus to continue his cause in the world.
- The resurrection is not some kind of juridical exchange between God and humanity brought about by the love of Jesus on the cross.
- The resurrection is not a divine intervention from outside, nor is it a suspension of the laws of nature.

If we are to take seriously the difficulties people have with resurrection, and if we are to move beyond the distortions just mentioned, then we must begin to relocate the resurrection within a larger framework. Part of the problem with understanding resurrection has been not only its isolation from the death of Jesus and from the preaching and praxis of Jesus, but also its separation from the larger story of creation. It is necessary, therefore, to relocate the resurrection within 'Big History'. This relocation requires that we take account of the new cosmic story embracing cosmology, biological evolution and the historical emergence of the human. Only within this expanded horizon can we begin to make some sense of the resurrection, rescue its rich meaning and recover its pivotal significance for eschatology. Further, the debate about resurrection must be relocated within the context of a robust theology of creation. For too long, the resurrection has been considered in isolation from creation.

To help with this relocation of the resurrection within the wider history of the cosmos, to reconnect the resurrection to creation and to re-establish the relationship between resurrection and the Spirit, we will invoke Karl Rahner's theology of grace. This theology of grace has had an overarching influence on the whole of Rahner's theology and is of particular significance for understanding the resurrection today. For Rahner, the grace of God in the world is informed by two related, but indivisible, moments. On the one hand, we have what Rahner calls God's gracious self-communication to the world, or as he puts it at times, God's self-bestowal on everything in the world. This action of God takes place from the dawn of time and is, therefore, present and active in the world from the beginning, and not as a once-off but as a continuous divine presence in the world. On the other hand, this action of God in the world affects the interiority, the very constitution of creation and humanity. The action of God's self-communication brings about a particular disposition and orientation within everything in the world. Rahner calls the effect of this divine presence in the world the gift of self-transcendence. Everything in the universe has an underlying orientation towards self-transcendence. This allows Rahner to talk about the graced self-transcendence of material creation, of life and of human beings. The self-bestowal of God on the world, given in the act of creation, brings about an inner dynamism of self-transcendence throughout the universe, not just on human beings but on the whole of material creation. Matter from the very beginning is graced with the gift of self-transcendence. There is no matter without grace, no grace without matter, no gift of the spirit without matter, no matter that is not without the spirit, as seen in Chapter 3.

For Rahner, this is the larger context in which we can begin to understand the new cosmic story. The story goes back some 13.8 billion years, beginning with the Big Bang and leading to the emergence of life some four billion years ago. From within life there is the emergence of the human 200,000 years ago as cosmic dust in a state of reflective self-consciousness. What is it that enables these transitions from matter to life, and from biological life to the emergence of reflective human beings? Rahner would answer that these shifts are the result of the ongoing presence of the endowment of creation *ab initio* with the gift and dynamism of self-transcendence. This gift of self-transcendence is made possible by the ongoing, enduring self-communication of the Spirit and Word of God throughout creation.

It is within this context of an expanding cosmology, the ongoing reality of biological life, and the continuous emergence of human beings as self-conscious matter that we should locate, in the first instance, the resurrection of Jesus. If these 'jumps' from cosmology to biology, and from biology to *Homo sapiens* are not a violation of the laws of nature, and are not the result of a divine intervention from outside, why then should we see the resurrection of Jesus as an interference from the outside?

Is it possible to locate the resurrection of Jesus within the dynamic continuum of the self-communication of God to the world and the ongoing self-transcendence of creation? Is it not possible to say that the resurrection of Jesus is a significant moment, a decisive transition in the history of the cosmos and biological life and human existence? These transitions do not require a divine intervention from the outside. On the other hand, it must be pointed out that they do require divine involvement. That divine involvement was initiated in the act of creation, which continues to be active in and through the gift of self-transcendence endowed on the whole of material creation and all human beings. This act of creation affects the interiority of material creation from the beginning.

In other words, it was in the act of creation that the possibility of resurrection was set in train. This orientation of creation towards new forms has manifested itself in various ways in the history of the cosmos, especially in the movements from matter to life and from biological life to human existence and from human life to the emergence of a new form of life, known as transformation and resurrection. As noted earlier, resurrection is best located within the divine act of creation. Creation has an inner orientation towards development and transformation and there are traces of this orientation towards new life within the history of the cosmos.

It is within this perspective that we can appreciate the observation by Denis Edwards when he points out perceptively that creation 'is eschatological from the ground up'.[13] Creation is tilted towards transformation from the beginning in virtue of the ongoing presence of the self-communication of God and the effect of that presence in terms of the self-transcendence that exists within creation itself. Similarly, for Elizabeth Johnson: 'Belief in the resurrection is a form of creation-faith'.[14] This link between creation and resurrection of course is captured explicitly in the Pauline description of the risen Christ as a New Creation. In the light of this relocation of resurrection within the larger context of evolutionary history, and the re-establishment of a close linkage between creation and resurrection, we can begin to make some symbolic statements about the meaning of resurrection.

The resurrection of Jesus is about the realisation of the potential for self-transcendence initiated by God's loving self-communication to the world 'in the beginning'. Resurrection is about the flowering forth of life within an evolutionary universe. Creation, graced by God from the beginning, is seeded with life, and this life comes to full bloom in the resurrection of Jesus from the dead. The realisation of self-transcendence, this flaring forth of new life in the risen Christ, is not an act of divine intervention from outside; instead, it is a bursting forth of new life within the universe that God intended and set in motion in the first act of creation.

This relationship between creation and resurrection mirrors the relationship between creation and Incarnation as one divine act which plays out in different phases, namely creation, resurrection and the ultimate consummation of creation in Christ. Creation is not resurrection, but it is the source of resurrection.

How, then, in the light of this biblical vision, and the new perspectives within *Laudato Si'*, might we begin to present a theology of resurrection that would promote the care of our common home in these times of an ecological emergency? To answer this question, the cosmic significance of resurrection can be outlined in a way that supports some of the questions raised at the beginning of this chapter. This will be followed with some remarks about the meaning of resurrection for understanding the human condition. These remarks will be influenced largely, but not exclusively, by Rahner's scattered reflections on resurrection.

1. The resurrection of Jesus from the dead is the 'beginning of the transformation of the world as an ontologically interconnected occurrence'.[15] The bodily resurrection of Jesus affects the whole body of material creation. As Paul puts it: the risen Christ is 'the first-born of all creation', 'the beginning, the first-born from the dead' (Colossians 1:15 and 18), and 'the first fruits of those who have died' (1 Corinthians 15:20 and 23). The import of this emphasis on the word 'first' is eschatological, pointing towards a turning point or breakthrough in history. This implies that the future of the world, the transformation of the universe, has already begun in the bodily resurrection of Jesus from the dead. By calling this eruption of new life 'an ontologically interconnected occurrence' Rahner is reminding us that we live in a unified, organically interconnected and interrelated world.

2. The resurrection of Jesus is 'the pledge … of the perfect fulfilment of the world'.[16] While the resurrection of Jesus is the realisation of a new moment in history, it is also at the same time a promise that something similarly new will happen to the rest of creation. The resurrection of Jesus, therefore, is a promise that involves not only humanity but the whole of creation. This cosmic character of the

resurrection is captured by Matthew when he describes the impact of the resurrection in apocalyptic symbols: the earth shaking, the rocks splitting, tombs being opened and bodies being raised up (Matthew 27:51–52).

3. The risen Christ is the 'representative of the new cosmos'.[17] This dense sentence will make sense only if and when we see Jesus as a child of the cosmos, as indeed every human being is a child of the cosmos. As the opening chapter of Genesis reminds us, the human (*adam*) is created out of the dust of the earth (*adamah)* and is, therefore, better understood as an 'earthling' or a 'worldling'. As an 'earthling', Jesus carries within himself elements of the cosmos, and those elements have been transformed in the bodily resurrection of Jesus from the dead. Further, we have seen that the human embodies the cosmos in a state of reflective self-consciousness and freedom. In this sense, the risen Christ embodies a part of the cosmos as transformed and so represents the new cosmos. This point is also captured by Paul when he describes the risen Christ as the last/final/ new Adam (1 Corinthians 15:45 and Romans 5:15 and 19).

4. The resurrection of Jesus is also about the adoption of the world by God through the action of the creative spirit. In the resurrection of Jesus, God takes unto himself the interior core of the universe and transforms that inner core of creation into a new creation. In this sense, the resurrection of Jesus from the dead is built into creation *ab initio.* A part of the material creation has been taken up into the eternal life of God. This adoption of the world by God began in the primordial act of creation (*creatio ex nihilo*) through the outpouring of the Spirit 'in the beginning'. This outpouring of the Spirit culminates in the resurrection as part of the one divine act of creation and will be consummated at the end of time for the whole of creation.

5. The resurrection represents the 'eschatological victory of God's grace in the world'.[18] The grace of God came into the world through the gift of creation (sometimes referred to as first grace). God's gracious self-communication to the world initiated the process of preparing a dwelling place appropriate for the Word to be enfleshed and to be at home. There is an underlying unity between creation and Incarnation but, more particularly, between creation and resurrection.

6. For Rahner, resurrection is like the first eruption of a volcano which shows that in the interior of the world God's fire is already burning and this will bring everything to blessed ardour in light.[19] This means that the future of the world, the transformation of the universe, has already begun. Yet it must be acknowledged that this future exceeds the capacity of the human imagination and can be spoken of only in symbols and stories.

These descriptions of resurrection are not so much distinct and different, but deliberately overlapping into mutually complementary aspects of a creation-centred understanding of resurrection. They are intended to widen the scope of resurrection from being exclusively anthropocentric to being also cosmo-centric. Another way of recovering these cosmic dimensions of resurrection is to apply Gregersen's principle of deep Incarnation as outlined in Chapter 4. Deep Resurrection is a resurrection that reaches into the roots of material and biological existence.

In seeking to recover the cosmic implications of resurrection one must not ignore the human implications of resurrection, of what some might call the anthropological significance of the bodily resurrection from the dead. Once again, we can only offer pointers to the meaning of resurrection for the human condition.

The individual and personal resurrection of Jesus from the dead is about the fulfilment of human hopes. Every human being hopes and agonises at some stage in life about the future. Many are plagued with questions about individual destiny: is human existence merely a puff of smoke, or a spark in the evolutionary spiral of life that one day will burn out and be no more? These and a host of other existential questions challenge faith in the resurrection of Jesus from the dead. More particularly, those who dare to affirm the resurrection of Jesus must engage with these questions, and allow their hope to be interrogated by such questions. Further, the resurrection of Jesus is about the completion of the human as unfinished, the overcoming of what is flawed about the human condition and the realisation of the unrestricted human desire to know and to love.

As Denis Edwards points out, the resurrection is about 'the instantiation of the potentialities that God has placed in the natural world from the beginning, potentialities that have always been directed towards resurrection and new creation'.[20] These human possibilities have been implanted in creation through the self-communication of God to the world *ab initio*, and the effect of that divine love is the gift of a dynamic self-transcendence within creation itself and human beings. The resurrection of Jesus, therefore, is about the personal fulfilment of the human self. In effect, the resurrection is the culminating moment of the gift of self-transcendence, bestowed on creation from the beginning of time.

This recovery of the cosmic significance of resurrection and the recognition that the new creation is not another *creatio ex nihilo*, but rather a *creatio ex vetere*, a recreation of the existing universe, has ecological implications. It highlights that the earth will be part of the new creation and, therefore, that the earth, all of the earth, creatures and non-human creatures, have their own intrinsic value. This puts an end to the damaging, utilitarian outlook on non-human creatures. Creatures, other than human, are not there to serve the needs of humanity, but rather have their own intrinsic goodness, value and integrity.

If this is the case, then non-human creation must be cultivated and respected in itself. In this way, eschatology can begin to bridge the gap between human beings and non-human creatures, between the human community and the community of creation, between society and the natural world. In addition, this relationship between human beings and non-human creatures begins to bring eschatology down to earth. It means that eschatology can now motivate our concern to develop the earth in its present form, or as the Second Vatican Council put it: 'The expectation of a new earth should spur us on' because, among other reasons, the cultivation of a this-worldly eschatology can give 'a foreshadowing in some way of the age that is to come'.[21]

To conclude these reflections on the relationship between eschatology and ecology it is important to acknowledge the place of theological humility when it comes to discourse about the resurrection and eschatology. We know very little about the future of the universe and how it will take place. Rahner, who had much to say about the future, none the less is very clear in pointing out that to think we could picture the future of the world in any detail 'would be more absurd than to suppose that the caterpillar could imagine what it would be like to be a butterfly'.[22] Part of the reason why Rahner is so insistent that we know so little about the future is because the future is about an encounter with the mystery of God, who remains incomprehensible. The Christ-event is as much a promise about the future as it is a revelation of what is to come. The revelation in Christ at most discloses the unity between death and resurrection. Further, the Christ-event discloses that the cross is at the centre of eschatology and that the shape of the future is cruciform, made up of a bright darkness, entailing a process of dying and rising, de-centring and re-centring. As Rahner points out, the role of eschatology is to act as the guardian of 'a learned ignorance about the future' (*docta ignorantia futuri*).[23] If we can see eschatology as already indicated, namely hope seeking understanding, then we can keep the future open. As Paul Ricoeur pointed out in the 1970s, hope is a protest against the premature closure of all systems of thought, especially religious and political fundamentalisms, as well as philosophical reductionisms and nihilisms.[24] Hope keeps thought and action open, and reacts against claims to absolute knowledge. All of hope, human, religious and Christian, is an impulse that resists closure and refuses finality, and this understanding of hope is also a way of reminding us of how little we know about the future. In emphasising the importance of 'learned ignorance' when it comes to eschatology, it is worth noting that Paul, who had so much to say about resurrection and a new creation in Christ, nonetheless insists that 'no eye has seen, nor ear heard, nor human heart conceived, what God has prepared for those who love him'

(1 Corinthians 29). Later on, in the same letter, Paul insists that 'now we see in a mirror dimly, but then we will see him face to face. Now I know only in part, then I will know fully, even as I have been fully known' (1 Corinthians 13:12).

CHAPTER 6

Ecology and Liturgy

AS IN the last couple of chapters, we will begin with some questions from ecology to liturgy, and from liturgy to ecology. The purpose of these questions is to raise awareness about the possible mutually critical interaction that could and should take place between ecology and liturgy in this era of a worsening climate crisis. More particularly, these questions intend to show how religion, ritual and the celebration of the Eucharist could have a role to play in tackling the global ecological emergency.

From ecology to liturgy, the following questions will arise. Can liturgy motivate worshipping communities to take more seriously their responsibility for the care of their common home? Is it possible for liturgy to build bridges with the wider ecological community of creation? How can liturgy engender a new ecological consciousness within the different parts of the liturgy? Is it possible for liturgy to take account of the pain and suffering of creation in the way that the Psalms in the Hebrew Bible do, and Paul does in the Letter to the Romans? How can liturgy foster a spirit of repentance for the 'sins' against the integrity of creation in the past and in the present? Is it possible for liturgy to unify the praise of nature for God within the praise of humans for God in the way that many psalms do?

Questions from liturgy to ecology include the following. How might ecology connect with the Liturgy of the Word and the Eucharist? Is it possible for ecology to suggest ways in which liturgy could embody a deeper ecological ethos and language? How might ecology help liturgy to recover its lost moorings in creation? How can ecology help the celebration of the Eucharist to connect more explicitly with the order, beauty, and wonders of creation? How can ecology enable the Eucharist to recover the foundational links that exist between creation and liturgy? Can ecology help liturgy to build a bridge between the celebration of the Eucharist and the natural world? These questions cannot be answered directly in a single short chapter, but an outline of some biblical and theological perspectives might open a new conversation between creation and liturgy.

One of the major problems facing liturgy today is the way it has become socially and culturally isolated from what is going on in the world, disconnected from ethical, spiritual and religious developments within the arts and humanities. More specifically, the celebration of the Eucharist has become separated internally from its original sources: in creation, in Passover, in the meal ministry of Jesus, in the actions of Jesus at the Last Supper, especially the washing of the feet, in the work of social and ecological justice, and in its connection to creation and eschatology. Again, these wide-ranging issues cannot be addressed here in any detail.[1] Instead, the focus will be on the recovery of some foundational links that exist between creation and liturgy, and between eucharist and ecology.

The Lost Link between Creation and Liturgy

One of the negative side effects of modernity, in spite of its many benefits, has been the isolation of liturgy from creation. In the pre-modern era, and going back to biblical times, and even further to pre-biblical times, there existed a close relationship between creation and liturgy. In pre-biblical times, a link existed between the ancient near-Eastern creation stories and the worship of gods, as in *The Epic of Creation (Enuma Elish)*. Within Judaism, a clear connection exists between creation and liturgy.

In the modern era there occurred what Charles Taylor has described as 'the disenchantment of the universe'. According to Taylor, 'Almost everyone can agree the big difference between us and our ancestors is that they lived in an enchanted world and we do not'.[2] The disenchantment of the universe resulted in the mechanisation of nature; some would say that it was the mechanisation of nature that gave rise to disenchantment. Prior to modernity, creation was experienced as a sacred place, a place permeated with a disarming presence of the divine. This numinous presence evoked a sense of mysteriousness about the universe in which people lived, something that was both overpowering and attractive at the same time – an experience captured by German theologian Rudolf Otto in his theology of the *mysterium tremendum et fascinans* in his book *The Idea of the Holy* (1904). This experience of the holy invited a sense of engagement and praise, gratitude and thanksgiving, awe and wonder, in relation to creation. The whole of the universe was experienced as teeming with an extraordinary and bewildering array of life: from matter to microbes to mammals. The sheer strangeness and otherness of the cosmos, of biological evolution and the appearance of humans within history, was a reminder that there is more going on in our universe than any human being could master. This experience of a numinous presence within the universe is reminiscent of Job's experience of creation in the latter part of the Book of Job. In spite of this experience of creation as both overpowering and fascinating, the mechanisation of nature ruled the day in modernity, with negative consequences. Nature was often reduced to the status of object, a product to be exploited by humanity for the use and benefit of human beings. With this mechanisation of nature, the earth lost its voice. Talk about nature was taken over by the language of science, the free market and economic efficiency. The voices of forests, 'wild' life and mountains were all silenced. Nature was diminished, de-personalised and discarded as empty matter. Animals were to be tamed, bred and farmed, often with little regard for their welfare, much less their intrinsic dignity. The human imagination was dulled and the relationship between human beings and nature was sidelined. The ancient links between nature and worship were severed. Creation was no longer experienced as a source of life and therefore no longer sensed as a gift. For many, nature was something to be controlled and manipulated, without much regard for its integrity. Nature was often portrayed as a threat to life, as a source of suffering and, therefore, something to be managed and dominated.

It may be helpful to show how the relationship between creation and liturgy was expressed in the Hebrew Bible. In the Jewish Psalter a clear link is evident in the experience of creation that resulted in the worship of Yahweh. For example, Psalm 95 is explicit in linking creation and worship:

> In His hand are the depths of the earth, the height of the mountains are His also. The sea is His, for He made it, and the dry land, which His hands have formed ...

> Oh come let us worship and bow down
> Let us kneel before the Lord, our master. (Psalm 95:4–6)

Psalm 104 begins with the verses:

> Bless the Lord, oh my soul.
> Oh Lord my God you are very good.

The Psalm goes on to outline in detail the work of creation with praise:

> You stretch out the heavens like a tent. (Psalm 104:2)

> You set the earth on its foundations
> You cover it with the deep as with a garment. (Psalm 104:5–6)

> You make the spring gush forth in the valleys. (Psalm 104:10)

> You cause the grass to grow for cattle
> And plants for people to use
> To bring forth food from the earth
> And wine to gladden the human heart, and oil to make the face shine, and bread to strengthen the human heart. (Psalm 104:5–15)

> You have made the moon to mark the seasons. (Psalm 104:19)

Then comes the response evoked by this wide-ranging experience of creation:

> May the glory of the Lord endure forever. (Psalm 104:31)

> I will sing to the Lord as long as I live
> I will sing praises to my God while I have my being
> May my meditation be pleasing to him, for I rejoice in the Lord. (Psalm104:31, 33–34)

The Psalm concludes as it began:

> Bless the Lord, O my soul,
> Praise the Lord! (Psalm 104:35)

These verses and others are examples of the influence that creation plays in bringing about prayer and worship of God as creator and redeemer of creation.

Lying behind these psalms is the presence of different theologies of creation. There are at least seven accounts of creation in the Hebrew Bible, and many others that are less developed. The formal seven accounts of creation can be found in:

> Genesis 1:1–2:3
> Genesis 2:4–3:24
> Job 38–41
> Psalm 104
> Proverbs 8:22–31
> Ecclesiastes 1:2–11; 12:1–7
> 2 Isaiah 40–55 (excerpts)[3]

In addition to the Psalms, a close relationship between creation and liturgy can be found in Genesis 1:1–2: 23. This opening chapter of the Bible 'enjoys pride of place ... among accounts of creation'. It is also understood as 'the cosmogony of cosmogonies' and is seen as 'the most carefully structured text in all of scripture'.[4]

In approaching Genesis, it is important that we do not expect answers to questions that would have been impossible to ask at that time, and alien to the culture of the composition of Genesis 1. The questions being addressed in the sixth century BCE are totally different from the questions that are asked today. Genesis does not answer questions raised by modern science, or modern cosmologies as understood by contemporary science, or biological evolution as developed by Charles Darwin.

One of the keys to a right interpretation of Genesis 1 is attention to its authorship. It is generally agreed among scholars that it was composed by the priests of the Jewish Temple and is known as the 'priestly account' of creation, going back to around the sixth century BCE. This particular background gives us a clue as to the purpose and intention of Genesis 1. The origins and context of this opening chapter in Genesis imply that it may have something to do with worship.

Another key to unlocking the significance of Genesis 1 is the structure of the text, which is both poetic and hymn-like. The text outlines the order and symmetry and beauty of creation. Further, Genesis 1 implies that this account of creation may have been recited in the Temple to the glory of God. References to creation as 'good', as 'very good', are surely an indication that this story of creation has something to do with thanking God for the goodness of creation. In addition, Genesis 1 deals with humanity's relationship to God, a relationship of gratitude. Moreover, the story of creation in Genesis 1 is carefully structured around seven days. The opening verses are made up of seven words; creation is pronounced good seven times; the number seven or multiples of seven appear in different passages. It is surely significant that the completion of creation takes place on the seventh day, which is declared as a day of rest, the sabbath. This closure of creation on the seventh day is not an after-thought, but rather a way of ensuring that the sabbath is an intrinsic part of the story. As one commentator says: 'The number seven conveys a ritual sense of completion or fulfilment'.[5]

In the light of these observations, there is a broad agreement among biblical commentators that Genesis 1 is about liturgy, and that this account of creation influenced the construction of the tabernacle and later the architecture of the Temple in Jerusalem. According to Terence

Fretheim, given 'the rhythmic cadences', in Genesis 1:1–2:3, 'this material has a doxological character and may have been honed in and through liturgical usage'.[6] Fretheim also holds that 'Worship interests also appear in links between this account and other texts associated with the tabernacle, Temple, Sabbath, and religious festivals'.[7] In addition, he holds that the style and structure of Genesis 1:1–2:24 was 'shaped by liturgical interests'.[8] Other commentators concur with Fretheim. For example, William P. Brown talks about 'the lofty liturgical cadences' within Genesis 1, which exist in contrast to the second creation account in Genesis 2:4–6; 3:24, which 'reads more (like) a Greek tragedy'.[9] A third commentator, Walter Brueggemann, holds that Genesis 1 sought to lift up the heavy hearts of a dispirited people in exile. The 'intent and effect of this liturgical narrative is to enact by its utterance a well-ordered, fully reliable, generative world for Israelites who are exiles in Babylon'.[10] Genesis is a counter-myth, so to speak, to the Babylonian creation myth, *Enuma Elish*.

Given this liturgical orientation of Genesis 1, creation is perceived and described as a 'cosmic temple',[11] as the 'throne of God' (Isaiah 66:1–2) and 'the sanctuary of God'.[12] Creation, therefore, is a sign, a symbol and a sacrament of the immanent presence of God in the world. To experience creation in all of its symmetry, beauty and complexity, is to experience something of the immanent presence of God in the world. For the people of Israel, the spirit of God dwells in creation. This presence of the Spirit in creation and the action of the Word of God in Genesis 1 and throughout the Bible is the basis of understanding creation as sacramental. It is this understanding of creation as Spirit-endowed that grounds the sacramental character of the Jewish liturgy in the tent, in the tabernacle and in the Temple. There is a fundamental principle at work here, both in Judaism and in Christianity. If we do not sense and experience the sacramental presence of the Spirit of God in creation, it is unlikely we will be able to encounter God in the liturgy of the Temple, or in the liturgy of the Christian Church – a principle we will return to in chapter 7, in the context of the Eucharist. If we lose contact with the sacramental character of the natural world, we lose contact with God. As Simon Oliver, the British theologian, puts it: 'If God is to be met in the temple made by human hands, this is only because God is first-met in the Temple of divine making, namely creation itself.'[13] Thus, the structure and order of the tabernacle and, eventually, of the Temple, is influenced by the structure and order of the creation narrative in Genesis 1:1–2:3.[14] This understanding of creation as the temple of God is also found in Philo of Alexandria (20 BCE–50CE) and in the Jewish-Roman historian, Josephus.[15]

To talk about creation as the 'Temple of God', as the 'Throne of God' and as the 'Sanctuary of God' is a clear recognition of the immanent presence of God in the world made possible by the outpouring of the Spirit and the action of the Word from the beginning of time, as already developed in the last chapter. It is this immanent presence of God in the world that helps us to realise that creation is not only the home of humanity, but also the dwelling place of God. As Ann Clifford sums up: 'The *oikos* is not only the household of life, but also the household of God. As the household of God, the *oikos* has an inherent sacrality, even a sacramentality.'[16]

A second distinguishing feature of Genesis 1 is that according to the surrounding culture, creation is the outcome of a conflict between competing gods. For instance, the creation epic *Enuma Elish* recounts the victory of the god Marduk. In Genesis, there is no such conflict or competition. Instead, the agent of creation in Genesis 1 is the one and only monotheistic God of Israel, who acts out of goodness.

A third distinguishing feature, already alluded to, is the emphasis on the seventh day, the sabbath, which marks the completion of creation. This seventh day is described as 'blessed and hallowed' because 'God rested from all the work he had done in creation' (Genesis 2:2–3). Much is lost when the story of creation is reduced to six days. Instead, the seventh day is 'the feast of creation', and is about resting in God, giving us a foretaste of the future and reminding us about the immanence of God throughout creation which comes into full view on the sabbath.[17] When reference to the sabbath is omitted, the liturgical character of Genesis is lost.

A further distinguishing feature of Genesis 1:1–2:3 is the references to humans having 'dominion over the fish of the sea, and over the birds of the air, and over the cattle and over all animals of the earth, over every creeping thing that creeps upon the earth' (Genesis 1:26). And this, in turn, is followed by a command to 'till the earth and subdue it; and have dominion over the fish' (Genesis 1:28). These references to humans having 'dominion' and subduing the earth are ambiguous and open to misinterpretation and manipulation. The ambiguity of these references has been coloured by their reception in the modern era, which interprets them as granting human beings permission and justification for the exploitation of the earth's resources for the exclusive use of human beings. Further, this textual ambiguity in Genesis 1 is compounded by the fact that many consider these references as being largely responsible for the ecological crisis today. Moreover, this apparent licence to dominate the earth has given humanity an exaggerated sense of its superiority over other creatures and an entitlement to stand outside the rest of creation.

When, however, we place Genesis 1 in the context of liturgy, we can see that the 'dominion' God gives should not be understood as untrammelled permission to exploit the natural world, but as an obligation to be wise. Humans created in the image of *Elohim* have to recognise God's goodness in creation and to respond by acting responsibly, not tyrannically nor selfishly, in our dominion as God does over the whole of creation.[18]

The overall effect of these few references in the Bible has had a disproportionate influence upon modern theologies of creation. Their impact has given rise to an anthropocentric understanding of creation in the modern era, with negative consequences for the way humans relate to the natural world. In addition to these negative effects, the teaching of Genesis 1 about humans as made in the image of God *(imago Dei)* is mistakenly and arrogantly perceived as further justification for our mastery and manipulation of, and tyranny over, creation.

These few references in Genesis 1:26–28 to dominion and subduing the earth have given rise to what is known as the 'dominion model of creation'. It should be noted that *Laudato Si'* is explicitly critical of the 'dominion model'. It is worth quoting the criticism here in full. The encyclical points out that the 'dominion model'

> has encouraged the unbridled exploitation of nature by painting him [man] as domineering and destructive by nature.

This is not a correct interpretation of the Bible as understood by the Church. Although it is true that we Christians have, at times, incorrectly interpreted the scriptures, nowadays we must forcefully reject the notion that our being created in God's image, and given dominion over the earth, justifies absolute dominion over creatures. (*LS*, 67)

These strong observations leave no doubt about the need to rethink the 'dominion model'. Before doing this, brief mention should be made of what is called the 'stewardship model' of creation.

The 'stewardship model' is an improvement on the 'dominion model'. It seeks to offer an alternative to the 'dominion model' and the domination and exploitation that it has produced. In recent times, there has been a critique of the 'dominion model' by a growing number of theologians, including Denis Edwards,[19] Richard Bauckham,[20] Elizabeth Johnson[21] and Dan Horan.[22] These theologians and others also argue persuasively that all is not well with the 'stewardship model' in spite of its good intentions. The underlying assumptions of the 'stewardship model' are problematic. They neglect the interdependence of the human species with the rest of life on earth; they see the human as independent and external and separate from the rest of creation; they establish a vertical, top-down relationship between humans and other creatures (effectively a hangover from the dominion model); they give humans a responsible mastery over other creatures, making them mere passive recipients.[23] In effect, the 'stewardship model' ends up promoting an anthropocentrism which gives humans control over and free use of the creatures of creation. In effect, the 'stewardship model' in practice is dualistic and hierarchical. These criticisms of the 'dominion model' and the 'stewardship model' beg the following question: can the original meaning of the 'dominion model' be retrieved?

For too many, there is all too often an easy and often unthinking slippage from dominion to domination. Furthermore, the reception of the 'dominion model' in the modern era, with its culture of individualism and consumerism, makes its retrieval nearly impossible today. In addition, the few isolated references to dominion in the Bible do not contain sufficient substance for self-critique. There is an emerging consensus that a new model, a new paradigm, is needed at this time to overcome dominion and domination. This new model of creation will go beyond the modern cult of individualism, the pervasive presence of anthropocentrism, the inflated views of human identity, and the relocation of human origins within the larger history of the cosmos. This new model will recognise the 'dominion model' as one note in the divine melody of creation. 'Dominion' is situated within the broader biblical theologies of creation found in the prophets, the Psalms and the Book of Job. This new model is variously described as a 'kinship model'[24] of creation, or the 'community of creation model'. We need to sketch an outline of what this new model looks like. What are the underlying characteristics of this new model of creation? What are the implications of this new model for the self-understanding of humanity?

The Community of Creation Model

This new model, or perhaps more accurately, this retrieval of the biblical vision of the community of creation, is first and foremost theocentric.

> The earth is the Lord's and all that is in it, the world and those who live in it. (Psalm 24: 1)

The community of creation is held together by the originating and ongoing creative action of the Spirit of God poured out at the dawn of time and accompanied by the presence of the Word of God, as seen in Chapter 3. Within this theocentric vision of creation, the whole of creation reflects its divine origins, and not just one particular part of creation. The whole of creation mirrors the creator and so, throughout the community of creation, there is a sacramental presence of the divine. This sacramental presence of God throughout creation is endorsed in the Genesis 1 story which culminates, not in the creation of the human but in the seventh day of the sabbath, a day of rest and a day set aside for prayer and worship. Further, the community of creation model relocates the dominion model within the wider theologies of creation in the Hebrew Bible.

A second feature of the community of creation is that it understands the place of the human within creation differently from that of the anthropocentrism found in the dominion model. This new model of the community of creation resituates the human being alongside other creatures within creation (e.g. Psalm 104). The community of creation sees other creatures as fellow creatures in the journey. Human beings are not above other creatures, but alongside other creatures, not separate from other creatures, but fellow creatures, not outside nature, but inside nature. As *Laudato Si'* says, humans 'are part of nature, included in it and thus in constant interaction with it' (*LS*, 139). This means moving away from an anthropocentric understanding of the universe into a radically theocentric world. This in turn requires that we see the human as part of a much larger story, part of a 'deep' time story which embraces an expanding cosmology, evolutionary biology and human emergence. There is a real difference in living as if one were external to that story as in the modern era, and living as interior to that story as required by the new cosmologies. The difference affects the self-understanding of human beings and heightens their moral responsibility for the *oikos* as insiders, and not just outsiders. Within this new perspective of human beings as members of the wider community of creation, we discover that humans need other species to survive. Human beings need clean air and water, fertile land and healthy trees to survive. Equally, other creatures need human beings to respect their internal life processes and integrity. Human beings are called to care for our common home, just as it cares for us.

A third characteristic of the community of creation is that there is a fundamental kinship, a fundamental alliance and affinity, between humans and other creatures. There exists, within the community of creation, a complex network which is profoundly relational. Everything in the community of creation is interrelated, interdependent and interconnected. This relationality of everything in the world can be found in a number of developments in the twentieth century, such as the process philosophy of Alfred Whitehead, in the many varieties of feminism, and in the different and new cosmologies. For example, according to Whitehead, our most primary experience is an experience of being part of, and belonging to, a larger continuum of past, present and future. There is a vague sense of the many which is one, and of the one which includes the many. For Whitehead:

> We are, each of us, one among others and all of us are embraced in the unity of the whole.[25]

Another striking example of this relational character of the universe, and especially of the relational unity between human beings and nature, can be found in Alice Walker's novel *The Color Purple*:

> My first step from the old white man (as God) was trees. Then air. Then birds. Then other people. But one day when I was sitting quiet, and feeling like a motherless child, which I was, it came to me: that feeling of being part of everything, not separate at all. I knew that if I cut a tree, my arm would bleed.[26]

This relational character of everything in the world, of economics and ecology, of nature and humans, of science and society, of social justice and ecological justice, is present throughout *Laudato Si'*.[27] The ultimate source of this radical relationality is attributed to the Trinity, 'who has left its mark on all creation' *(LS, 239)*.

There are different, but complementary, ways in which the action of the Trinity can be articulated: descending and ascending models. In the former, God the Father creates all things in the Spirit through the Word. In the latter, the Spirit of God is poured out 'in the beginning' through the Word to reveal the Father.[28] The latter model is the preferred point of departure in developing a theology of the community of creation: it highlights the action of the Spirit throughout the whole of creation from the beginning. A Spirit-driven theology of creation grounds the interconnectedness, interrelationality and interdependence of everything in the world.

A fourth characteristic of the community of creation brought out imaginatively by Elizabeth Johnson is that within this community of creation we have new neighbours. Within the community of creation, the notion of neighbour extends beyond the human species to include other living creatures and the vibrant life of the natural world. Consistent with this emphasis on new neighbours within the wider community of creation, Johnson goes on to say we need to broaden the boundaries of our pronouns. When we talk of 'we' or 'us' or 'you', we should include our new neighbours in the earth community within the range of meaning and reference. This adjustment to our new neighbours, and the widening of the range of reference should apply to all thought, speech, teaching, preaching and prayer, except in those instances where reference is exclusive to human beings. This will require a new way of being, a new way of thinking, a new way of acting in the world and a new way of worshipping. Johnson describes this adjustment as the new 'ecological vocation'[29] for humanity in the twenty-first century.

In promoting this new paradigm, reference so far has been to the Hebrew Bible. What about the New Testament? And, in particular, what about the teaching of Jesus regarding creation? Commentators point out that the religious imagination of Jesus was deeply grounded in the world of nature and rooted in the traditions of Israel.[30] Further, it is noted that Jesus employs different parables to communicate the multi-layered meaning of the coming reign of God. Many of these parables employ stories about human beings, but most of these stories are about nature and the lives of other than human creatures within nature. It could be said that the wider community of creation is invoked by the imagination of Jesus in his discourse about the reign of God. It is possible to distinguish here between stories about the animal world and the natural world as invoked by Jesus to teach something of the depth and breadth and length of the coming reign of God. Richard Bauckham lists the following animals as mentioned by Jesus: birds, camels, chickens, dogs, donkeys, doves, fish, foxes, gnats, goats, moths, oxen, pigs, ravens, scorpions, sheep, snakes, sparrows, vipers, vultures and wolves. Alongside the animals, there are also many references to the life of nature: brambles, fig trees, herbs, mulberries, mustard plants, reeds, thorns, vines, weeds, wheat and wild flowers.[31] This wide range of references to the larger community of creation is striking by any standard. These references suggest that the community of creation, as made up of humans, other creatures and the vibrant life of nature, are different metaphors for understanding the reign of God. Look at the active life of creation and you will get a glimpse of the reign of God.

Further, it should not be forgotten that Jesus taught his disciples to pray in the following way:

> Our Father in heaven
> Hallowed be your name
> Your kingdom come,
> Your will be done,
> On earth as it is in heaven
> (Matthew 6:9–10)

It will be clear, at this stage, that there is an extraordinary range of diversity within the community of creation, and yet this diversity has its origin and source in the enduring action of the Spirit (Psalm 104). This unity within creation is supported and sustained by the ongoing creative action of the Spirit in humans, in other creatures, and the life of nature. At the same time, the Word of God structures this extraordinary diversity within the community of creation. Where the Spirit is active, there is unpredictable diversity breaking out, and yet at the same time, this diversity is structured and ordered by the Word/*Logos*. As seen already, Spirit/*Pneuma* and Word/*Logos* work in tandem (Psalm 38). Creativity and order, innovation and structure, are hallmarks of the community of creation.

What is significant in these examples is that the community of creation, the life of creation, is a primary symbol of the reign of God. To encounter the diversity of creation is to get a glimpse into the multi-layered meaning of the reign of God. For the sake of completion on this point, reference must also be made to the creation-centred Christologies of Paul, the Pauline literature, and the Prologue of John's Gospel, as outlined in Chapter 4. In noting this unity of the creative and the structured, we must ask the question (a question that is outside the scope of this book): Is there some echo here between the creative action of the Spirit and the structured presence of the Word on the one hand, and the interplay that exists within biological evolution between chaos and order on the other?

Within this outline of the community of creation model, in contrast to the narrowly anthropocentric interpretation of the dominion model, it needs to be noted that a significant shift in our understanding of the human is being proposed. The human exists within the community of other creatures. Further, it must be acknowledged that the human and other creatures have much in common. Given their shared origins, through the action of the Spirit in the beginning, and their shared destiny in the New Creation in Christ, this similarity between humans and other creatures should not surprise us. Most would agree with Elizabeth Johnson in her observation that

> Humanity and other species have more in common than what separates them.[32]

This statement is supported by the scientific claim that humans and other creatures share a very similar structure of DNA. This relocation of the human within the community of creation begs a number of questions that must, at least, be noted: Does the community of creation model dissolve the uniqueness of humanity assumed by the anthropocentrism of the dominion model? Is there a certain anthropological reductionism at play here, even a whiff of creaturely levelling and relativism? Have we ended up dumbing down what is distinctive about the human being?

To begin to answer these concerns about human uniqueness, we need to recap some of the features of the community of creation. The primary emphasis is that everything within the community of creation is theocentric in different ways and to varying degrees, that is, creation comes from God, is a gift from God, and returns to God in the fullness of time. This theocentric feature refers to the whole of creation, and not just human beings. All of creation is centred in God, through the indwelling of the Spirit of God. This shifts the centre of gravity within creation from humans as the exclusive holders of the *imago Dei*. All of creation, and not just humans, is in the image of God. Aquinas asks whether God is present in all things. He says:

> God is present in all things; not indeed as part of their essence, not as an accident, but as an agent is present to that upon which it works.

He continues: 'Therefore as long as a thing has being, God must be present to it, according to its mode of being'.[33] Aquinas continues this discussion in the next article of the *Summa*:

> For God brought things into being in order that His goodness might be communicated to creatures, and be represented by them; and because this goodness could not be adequately represented by one creature alone, he produced many and diverse creatures, that what was wanting to one in the representation of divine goodness, might be supplied by another.[34]

The point that Aquinas is making is that no one particular creature, not even the human, can adequately image God by itself.[35] Thus, the community of creation, in all its diversity, better images God more than any one human being.[36] Here we see a shift from a purely anthropocentric universe to a theocentric universe. Within this diversity of creation, there are differences, distinctions and relationships, but these are not absolute. As Leslie Muray sums up:

> The difference between humans and non-humans is a matter of degree and not of kind.[37]

The only absolute difference within the community of creation is the difference between the transcendence of God and creation, between God and the world. Respect for differences within the community of creation is important, and this respect for the diversity of creation allows for individual differences, distinctiveness, and singularities without losing what is unique within the community of creation and without levelling the range of individual differences to the lowest common denominator. In other words, the uniqueness of human beings and non-human beings derives from their relational origin and their relational destiny within the divine plan, as well as varying degrees of reflective self-consciousness, different capacities to bring the past into the present through the power of memory, and diverse abilities to anticipate the future through the creativity of the imagination.

What is distinctive and unique about the diversity within the community of creation is not the superiority of one over the other, nor the separation of one from others; instead what is distinctive is the unique relationship that exists between creator and creation, between God and the different entities of world. This unique relationship derives from the origin of creation in the creator. This relationship from the side of the community of creation is a relationship orientated towards the creator. To exist is to co-exist, to be is to be in relationship with God, being/*esse* is being towards the creator (*esse ad creatorem*). This relationality of creatures towards the creator is described by Aquinas as one of participation by creatures, all creatures, in God as the source of being. There is, therefore, a distinction between God and creation and, at the same time, a relationship of participation and togetherness and dependency between creation and the creator, between God and creatures. In moving from dominion to the community of creation, we are not moving from anthropocentrism to bio-centrism, but from anthropocentrism to a theocentric understanding of the whole of creation and, in particular, towards a theological anthropology.[38] Further, this reconfiguration of the distinctively human within the larger context of the wider community should not be understood as diminishing the dignity of the human within the larger context of creation.

To conclude, the model of the community of creation opens up new avenues for understanding liturgy. Unlike the 'dominion' and 'stewardship models', it does not place the human at the centre or above nature, but nests humanity in creation. In a post-modern world it may be romantic to try to simply recover the enchanted realm of the pre-modern world. Yet the 'big history' can evoke a new sense of wonder.

We are part of a 13.8 billion-year story. It is not merely a story of inanimate matter, but always in-spirited, graced matter, as we saw in Chapter 5. The intrinsic relations of all there is grounds the imagination that liturgy needs. The divine is not immanent in particular enchanted things, places, people or cloud-dwelling divinities. Rather, the whole of the cosmos presents the creator to us. We are inextricably linked with all there is. We are composed of the ashes of stars. All the 'stuff' that is here and now was present there and then at the very beginning.

In general, liturgies are community events. If humanity is the universe becoming conscious of itself, then liturgies are the universe as a community of creation praising God. Liturgy is not separate from the rest. It is not the action of a celebrant alone, or even of the human community alone. It is the voice of the universe praising the one who called it all into being (*LS*, 89). Good liturgy enables us to discover who we truly are.

This outlook on what is happening in the liturgy, namely the whole of creation praising God, changes the relationship between humans and creation from being one of domination to one of kinship/affinity, from exploitation to respect, and from competition to cooperation in communion. This is a significant shift. It means that the uniqueness of the human cannot be argued for at the expense of the community of creation. It is no longer a question of affirming the uniqueness of human beings over and against creation. Instead, it is about affirming the distinctiveness of both humans and other creatures in a way that is complementary and not oppositional. Humans and other creatures hold too much in common to be pitted against each other: shared origins through the outpouring of the Spirit and a shared destiny in becoming part of the New Creation in Christ.

Laudato Si' is conscious that there is a danger of misunderstanding within this shift and so it goes out of its way to state clearly:

> This is not to put all living beings on the same level, nor to deprive human beings of their unique worth and the tremendous responsibility it entails. (*LS*, 90)

Equally, it does not 'imply a divinisation of the earth which would prevent us from working on it in its fragility' (*LS*, 90). Such extreme views 'end up creating new imbalances' (*LS*, 90). In stating what *is not* the case, *Laudato Si'* is moving a little closer to what *is* the case. Clearly, further refinement is required of this key question of what is distinctive about human identity within the larger community of creation.[39]

CHAPTER 7

Laudato Si' and the Cosmic Eucharist

THE SHIFT from the dominion model to a community of creation model needs further elaboration. In particular, it requires the support of a renewed theology of the natural world. For too many centuries, the natural world has been objectified by modern science and neglected by theology. Forty years ago Carolyn Merchant wrote an important book on *The Death of Nature*.[1] Charles Taylor has described the shift from an enchanted world to a 'disenchanted universe'. Others talk about the 'desacralisation' of the world. In the light of the ecological crisis, the shift from dominion to a community of creation and the necessary critique of anthropocentrism, there is now an urgent need for a new theology of the natural world. A theology in which the natural world is foundational to the community of creation is essential background to understanding the cosmic Eucharist. More specifically, there is a need to reimagine the relationship of humans with nature, no longer as masters but as companions, no longer as exploiters but as carers, no longer as tourists passing through but as residents with shared responsibilities. And, equally, it is important to reimagine the relationship between the natural world and the cosmic Eucharist.

A Theology of the Natural World as Essential Background to the Cosmic Eucharist

Is it possible to begin to see the natural world as a dwelling place of the Spirit of God? How can we overcome the mistaken view that God is an absentee landlord in the natural world? Can we discover that, at the core of creation, there is a divine and deeply spiritual hallmark? Is it possible to experience nature as a place where the gracious presence of God breaks into our lives from time to time, to disclose that we are already part of a grace-filled naturalism?[2] Can we go beyond the mechanisation, materialisation and objectification of nature brought about by modern science? Is it possible to experience nature as symbolic and sacramental? In brief, is the re-enchantment of the universe possible in the twenty-first century, in a way that builds on the enchantment of the universe in the pre-modern era and, at the same time, takes account of scientific developments in the present? These questions, it is hoped, capture a little of the magnitude of the challenge facing theology today in terms of an appreciation of the natural world. Clearly these questions cannot be answered in this chapter. At most, we can only intimate some theological principles that point a way forward.

The criteria for selecting these principles will be twofold. In the first instance, we will seek to map out what a theology of the natural world might look like. Secondly, this theology of the natural world will seek to build a bridge between the natural world and liturgy, and in particular between the natural world and the celebration of the Eucharist that overcomes the isolation of the Eucharist from creation.

This chapter seeks to reconnect Eucharist and creation in a way that echoes the link between creation and worship in biblical times. To do this, it will be necessary to recover the symbolic and sacramental character of nature. Without a renewed appreciation of the inner and dynamic life of the natural world, the sacramental life of some religions, and especially the sacramental life of the churches, will be increasingly irrelevant, and the place of the Eucharist within creation and its relationship to ecology will be lost.

Laudato Si' outlines a number of theological principles that prompt a renewed theological appreciation of the natural world. The first of these principles is that we approach nature as a book to be read. *Laudato Si'* points out that 'God has written a previous book whose letters are the multitude of created things present in the world' (*LS*, 85). Other references to nature as a book can be found scattered throughout the document (*LS*, 6, 12 and 239). Nature as a book, and therefore as a text to be interpreted, does not interpret itself. It is like any other text – open to different interpretations; in the biblical tradition alone, many interpretations of creation are possible. Indeed, the text of nature is ambiguous, at times evoking awe and wonder, especially in view of the complex networks throughout nature in terms of cooperation, interdependence and interconnectedness. On the other hand, this particular view of nature must be balanced by the presence of competition, suffering, terror and violence, summed up in words attributed to Alfred Lord Tennyson (1809–1892) that nature 'is red in tooth and claw'. In between these two interpretations of the book of nature is the presence of a recurring cycle of life and death, and death and rebirth.

In reading the book of nature in the twenty-first century, we have at our disposal resources that were never available before: magnified microscopes, telescopes and nano-technology. Through the findings of the sciences, especially the new cosmologies, quantum physics and biological evolution, we can see things that were never seen before in the modern era. Modern science opens up new vistas, new questions, requiring careful scrutiny and interpretation.

This understanding of nature as a book is not new; it has been present in the Judaeo-Christian tradition. A good example can be found in Saul, the Jew, drawing on his Jewish theology of creation, and Paul, the Christian, influenced by the Christ-event. Paul could write:

> Ever since the creation of the world, his eternal power and divine nature, invisible though they are, have been understood and seen through the things he has made. (Romans 1:20)

In the life of the early Church, and in the Middle Ages, nature was seen as a resource for learning more about the human condition, and about the place of humans in the natural order, and their relationship to creation and the Creator. In a well-known quotation, Augustine suggests:

> Some people, in order to discover God, read a book. But there is a great book: the very appearance of created things. Look above and below, note, read. God whom you want to discover,

did not make the letters with ink; he put in front of your eyes the very things that he made. Can you ask for a louder voice than that?[3]

This approach to nature as a book to be read and interpreted is also found in Aquinas, Bonaventure and the Franciscans.

Within this tradition of reading the book of nature, it was not just idle curiosity, but rather a deep appreciation 'that nature was a resource for learning about humanity and its place in the cosmic hierarchy'.[4] In this regard, one need only think for a moment about how much nature has taught humanity about medical science, about the caring and healing of the whole community of creation. However, in the light of the ambiguous character of nature, and the incompleteness of nature, it is necessary to recover and interpret the book of nature beside the Bible. This brings us to the second principle in constructing a theology of the natural world.

Laudato Si', quoting the Canadian bishops, says that nature is 'a constant source of wonder and awe' and 'also a continuing revelation of the divine' (*LS*, 85). A few paragraphs later, it notes how the Brazilian bishops 'have pointed out that nature, as a whole, not only manifests God but is also a locus of his presence. The Spirit of life dwells in every living creature, and calls us to enter into a relationship with him' (*LS*, 88, see also 80 and 238). The 'contemplation of creation allows us to discover in each thing the teaching which God wishes to hand on to us' (*LS*, 85). In this context, *Laudato Si'* urges us to read the Bible with the book of nature: 'alongside revelation properly so-called, contained in the sacred scripture, there is a divine manifestation in the blaze of the sun and the fall of night' (*LS*, 85).

A third theological principle in *Laudato Si'* is the emphasis on communion within nature. The encyclical talks about 'a sublime' *(LS,* 89), 'deep' (*LS*, 91) and 'universal' communion that exists throughout the natural world (*LS*, 88). This communion that permeates the natural world is based on an ecological, philosophical and theological understanding of the natural world as interrelated, interconnected, and interdependent (*LS*, 120, 117, 137, 138, 141, 142). This understanding recognises the competition and conflict in the material world, but these presume the shared, communal world of nature. This emphasis on communion echoes a similar emphasis by Thomas Berry (1914–2009) back in the 1980s: 'The universe is not a collection of objects but a communion of subjects.'[5]

This sense of 'sublime communion' is grounded in 'our conviction that, as part of the universe, called into being by the one Father, all of us are linked by unseen bonds and together form a kind of universal family' (*LS*, 89). Being part of this universal family, we are filled 'with a sacred, affectionate, and humble respect' for the natural world and so 'we can feel desertification of the soil almost as a physical ailment, and the extinction of a species as a painful disfigurement'. Further, this 'deep communion' with the rest of nature 'cannot be real if our hearts lack tenderness, compassion, and concern for our fellow human beings' (*LS*, 91). As we saw in Chapter 2, the way we treat each other reflects the way we treat the natural world and vice versa.

A fourth principle in *Laudato Si'* is the recognition of 'the world as a sacrament of communion' (*LS*, 9). The communion that underlies nature adds up to an understanding of nature as a symbol and sacrament of communion. This in turn enables us to see that 'the divine and the human meet in the slightest detail in the seamless garment of God's creation, in the last speck of dust of our planet' (*LS*, 9). This focus on the existence of communion within the natural world and the suggestion that nature is a sacrament of communion has a number of advantages. It points us towards the possibility of a re-enchantment of the universe. It recovers something of the symbolic and sacramental character of nature. It echoes the biblical understanding of creation as the Temple of God, or the Throne of God or the Sanctuary of God, as seen earlier in the biblical theology of creation in the Psalms, and especially in Genesis 1. In this way, *Laudato Si'* lays an important foundation for recovering the link between liturgy and creation and, in particular, between ecology and Eucharist.

A fifth principle enunciated in *Laudato Si'* that can contribute to a renewed theology of the natural world is that:

- other creatures 'have value in themselves'; (*LS*, 33)
- other living beings 'have a value of their own in God's eyes'; (*LS*, 69)

- other species are not 'subordinate to the good of human beings as if they had no worth in themselves' (*LS*, 69).

In contrast, *Laudato Si'* teaches that other creatures 'have an intrinsic value independent of their usefulness' (*LS*, 140). This appreciation of the intrinsic value of other species is regarded by some as breaking new ground in Catholic teaching.[6]

There are a number of theological reasons underlying this new appreciation of the intrinsic value of other creatures. First of all, other creatures are, as already seen, 'a locus' of God's presence *(LS*, 88). For the encyclical, the 'Spirit of life dwells in every living creature and calls us to enter into a relationship with him' *(LS*, 88). Once again, we see how foundational pneumatology is to ecology and the teaching of *Laudato Si'*. Another reason why other species have value in themselves is because 'Creation is of the order of love' and this love of God is 'the fundamental moving force in all created things' (*LS*, 77). In this context the encyclical refers to the words of Dante Alighieri, who speaks of 'the love which moves the sun and the stars' (*LS*, 77). Moreover, other creatures have value in themselves because all of creation is destined for a new life in the Risen Christ: 'all creatures are moving forward with us and through us towards a common point of arrival ... where the Risen Christ embraces and illumines all things' (LS, 83). In the light of this new appreciation of the natural world, we can move to the second part of this chapter, which deals with the cosmic Eucharist.

Different Dimensions to the Cosmic Eucharist
It may be helpful to frame our discussion about the cosmic Eucharist by noting prescient observations of Mircea Eliade (1907–1986) some sixty years ago concerning challenges facing Christianity:

> As for the Christianity of the industrial societies and especially the Christianity of intellectuals, it has long since lost the cosmic values it still possessed in the Middle Ages. The cosmic liturgy, the mystery of nature's participation in the Christological drama, have become inaccessible to Christians living in a modern city ... at most we recognise that we are

responsible to God and also to history – but the world is no longer felt as the work of God.[7]

There are a number of issues present in these dense sentences which should be kept in mind as we look at *Laudato Si'* on the Eucharist. Eliade is pointing out that Christianity for the intellectuals has lost the cosmic values it once had. He is also suggesting that cosmic liturgy should include nature's participation in the Christological drama, that is, nature's participation in the drama of the historical death and resurrection of Jesus as the Christ. And, thirdly, for Eliade, the cosmic liturgy has become inaccessible for Christians living in a modern city today. With the Internet and all its connections, the whole world has become 'urbanised' in this sense. Save for those who drop out, we are all urbanites. These observations of Eliade are a succinct summary of the challenges facing ecology and the cosmic Eucharist in the twenty-first century.

By way of introduction to the encyclical's explicit treatment of the Eucharist, *Laudato Si'* offers two broad principles about the sacraments in general. 'The sacraments are a privileged way in which nature is taken up by God to become a means of mediating supernatural life' (*LS*, 235). In other words, the sacraments are about the lifting up of nature to a new theological level or, as is often stated, 'grace builds on nature' and therefore does not bypass nature. The second principle is that in and through 'our worship of God we are invited to embrace the world on a different plain' (*LS*, 235). The sacraments light up the value and symbolic significance of nature, inviting us to see our common home with its complex ecological networks in a new light, and appreciate the presence of the divine in the elements of the universe, especially the unique presence of Christ in a fragment of matter.

Explicit references to the Eucharist occur towards the end of *Laudato Si'* (*LS*, 235–37). As such, these references are scattered and are not intended to be an exercise in systematic theology. Yet, they do contain the seeds of a systematic theology on the Eucharist. For that reason, we will group the statements systematically into different, but complementary, categories:

Theocentric Dimensions of the Eucharist

In celebrating the Eucharist:

- 'Creation is projected towards divinisation, towards the holy wedding feast, towards unification with the Creator himself.' (*LS*, 236)
- 'Sunday, like the Jewish Sabbath, is meant to be a day which heals our relationships with God, with ourselves, with others and with the world.' (*LS*, 237)
- God 'comes not from above, but from within … that we might find him in this world'. (*LS*, 236)

Christocentric dimensions of the Eucharist

In celebrating the Eucharist:

- 'Sunday is the day of resurrection, the first day of the new creation, whose first fruits are the Lord's risen humanity, the pledge of the final transfiguration of all created reality.' (*LS*, 237)
- 'The Lord, in the culmination of the Mystery of the Incarnation, chose to reach our intimate depths through a fragment of matter.' (*LS*, 236)

Creation-centred dimensions of the Eucharist

In celebrating the Eucharist:

- 'All that has been created finds its greatest exaltation.' (*LS*, 236)
- We discover 'the living centre of the universe, the overflowing core of love and of inexhaustible life'. (*LS*, 236)
- 'Heaven and earth' … 'joins'. (*LS*, 236)
- 'All creation' is embraced. (*LS,* 236)

Cosmo-centric dimensions of the Eucharist

In celebrating the Eucharist:

- 'The whole cosmos gives thanks to God. Indeed, the Eucharist is itself an act of cosmic love.' (*LS* 236)
- When 'celebrated on the humble altar of a country church, the Eucharist is always in some way a celebration on the altar of the world'. (*LS* 236)

Eco-centric dimensions of the Eucharist
In celebrating the Eucharist:
- 'Through our worship of God, we are invited to embrace the world on a different plane.' (*LS*, 235)
- We have 'a source of life and motivation for our concerns for the environment, directing us to be stewards of creation'. (*LS*, 236)
- We are motivated 'to greater concern for nature and the poor'. (*LS*, 237)

These quotations from the encyclical are not intended to be a theological treatise on the Eucharist. Rather, they are pointers within the encyclical prompting further liturgical and theological reflection on the Eucharist. They overcome the isolation of the Eucharist from life and the rest of theology; they highlight the link between Eucharist and creation; they point up the relationship between Eucharistic and ecological concerns. Here we see the relocation of the Eucharist within the story of creation in a way that resonates with the biblical link between creation and the Temple of God as outlined earlier on. Further, the Eucharist points to the future of the *cosmos* (in the *eschaton*) when God will be all in all. In addition, the Eucharist motivates us to be concerned about the environment, nature and the poor. Moreover, the Eucharist is the source of healing our relationships with God, ourselves, others and the earth.

This new theology of the Eucharist has a background, immediately in the writings of his papal predecessors, and more remotely in the pioneering work of Teilhard de Chardin.[8]

Some will be surprised to know that Paul VI, St John Paul II and Benedict XVI, each in their own way, expressed appreciation of the work of Teilhard de Chardin, especially in relation to the Eucharist. It should be remembered that Teilhard was not allowed to publish his writings while he was alive. It was only after his death, in 1955, that most of his writings were published and made available publicly, just in time for the Second Vatican Council, at which he had some direct and indirect influence, especially in *Gaudium et Spes* (*The Pastoral Constitution on the Church in the Modern World*). It should also be noted that Teilhard gets a footnote in *Laudato Si'*, which acknowledges 'the contribution of Fr.

Teilhard de Chardin' to our understanding of creation and Christ (*LS*, 83, n.53).

On 24 February 1966, Paul VI gave an address to workers in a chemical and pharmaceutical plant, in which he referred, with caution, to the work of Teilhard.

More explicit are the reflections of St John Paul II and Benedict XVI, both of whom adopt the vision and language of Teilhard's 'Mass on the World' (1923).[9] In 1996, St John Paul II wrote:

> Eucharist is also a celebration in order to offer on the altar of the whole earth the world of work and sufferings in the beautiful words of Teilhard de Chardin.[10]

In addition, St John Paul II, in his encyclical on the Eucharist, refers again to Teilhard. Reflecting on his experiences of celebrating the Eucharist, he notes they have

> given me a powerful experience of its universal and, so to speak, cosmic character. Yes, cosmic! Because, when it (that is, the Eucharist) is celebrated on the humble altar of a country church, the Eucharist is always a celebration on the altar of the world.[11]

Benedict XVI also positively acknowledges Teilhard's vision. On 15 June 2006, in a homily marking the Feast of Corpus Christi, he pointed out that

> Liturgy may not be something alongside the reality of the world, but that the world itself shall become a living host, a liturgy. This is also the great vision of Teilhard de Chardin: in the end we shall achieve a true cosmic liturgy, where the *cosmos* becomes a living host.[12]

On 24 July 2009, during a celebration of Vespers in the cathedral of Aosta, Italy, Benedict, at the end of a reflection on Romans 8, says:

It is the great vision [of Paul in Romans] that later Teilhard de Chardin also had. In the end, we will have a true cosmic liturgy, where the *cosmos* becomes a living host. Let us pray to the Lord that He helps us to be priests in this sense, to help in the transformation of the world, in the adoration of God, beginning with ourselves.[13]

Behind these quotations on the Eucharist in *Laudato Si'* and the quotations taken from St John Paul II and Benedict XVI, is the influential writing of Teilhard de Chardin, especially his reflections on 'The Mass on the World' (1923). This essay is a deeply personal, symbolic and poetic reflection on the relationship between Eucharist and the *cosmos*. In the opening paragraph, he tells us how he found himself in the trenches of the First World War (1917), and again in the Ordos Desert in China, without the basic ingredients for the celebration of the Eucharist: 'I have neither bread, nor wine, nor altar'.[14] What is he to do to fulfil his desire to celebrate the Eucharist? 'I will raise myself beyond these symbols up to the pure majesty of the real itself; I, your priest, will make the whole earth my altar, and on it I will offer you the labours and sufferings of the world'. He continues: 'I will place, on my patten, O God, the harvest to be won by this renewal of labour. Into my chalice I shall pour all the sap which is to be pressed out of this day from the earth's fruits.' He goes on in this mystical vision to talk about matter and spirit, light and darkness, and fire (representing the Spirit). In addition, he discusses the immensity of the cosmos, the unity and community of all that makes up the universe, surrender, self-sacrifice and transformation, and the human as a microcosm.[15] This is an essential part of the background to understanding the teaching of *Laudato Si'* on the Eucharist, and the influence of St John Paul II and Benedict XVI on the Eucharist in *Laudato Si'*, both of whom are quoted and footnoted in paragraph 236.

Within these few paragraphs, Pope Francis is outlining *in nuce* a programme for the renewal of liturgical celebration and eucharistic theology. He is endorsing the relatively new emphasis on the cosmic character of the Eucharist; he is recognising the ancient link between creation and liturgy; he is affirming the relationship that can, and should, exist between eucharist and ecology; he is presenting the Eucharist as a motive for a new ecological praxis in relation to the environment, nature and the poor. Our Eucharistic theology is deficient in so far as it neglects to explore these emphases and exemplify how to put them into practice.

Equally important is the way Teilhard, St John Paul II, Benedict XVI and Francis have opened up the possibility for the celebration of the Eucharist within the larger context of the unfolding of the universe, the evolution of all life on planet earth, and the recent emergence of the human within the larger history of 13.8 billion years. Many people live out their lives in the context of a progressive/evolutionary outlook on the world. If this outlook is not reflected within the vision and language of liturgy, more and more people will feel ill at ease at Sunday Eucharist, and will simply walk away.

Reference should be made here to an ancient liturgical principle that 'the way one prays influences what one believes', known as the *lex orandi, lex credendi*, a principle that goes back to the fifth century. The reception of this principle down the years suggests that the movement from prayer to belief can also go from belief to prayer. The point at issue here is that the worship and belief should influence each other, and that neither can ignore the developments of contemporary science.[16]

Many would hold that the advances of contemporary science offer more reasons – not fewer – for cultivating a life of prayer and worship. For instance, discoveries of the new cosmologies and physics open extraordinary levels of beauty, order and symmetry in the *cosmos* which, until recently, were unknown in the fine detail available to us today. These experiences evoke responses of awe and wonder, amazement and humility, praise and gratitude. It is responses like these that are at the heart of prayer and the foundation of worship for many.[17] It has been the genius of Teilhard to show how cosmology can enhance and deepen the meaning of the Eucharist. *Laudato Si'* has brought the insights of Teilhard to a new level by linking the celebration of the Eucharist with ecological praxis in the service of our common home.

What does it mean then to talk about the cosmic Eucharist? In what sense is the Eucharist linked to the cosmos? How does the Eucharist relate to the 'cosmic liturgy' and the 'Christological drama' mentioned by Eliade? For Teilhard, there is a link between the Eucharist and the cosmos. The Eucharist must not be isolated from what is going on in the larger life of the universe. We must learn to see that 'the Host of bread is continually encircled more closely by another, infinitely larger Host, which is nothing less than the universe itself ... the world is the final and the real Host into which Christ gradually descends, until His time is fulfilled'.[18]

This quote from Teilhard will not make much sense unless we realise, as US theologian John C. Haughey points out, that 'Teilhard spent much of his life seeing wholes operating in the universe'.[19] Examples of seeing wholes would be the relationship Teilhard sees between cosmo-genesis, anthropo-genesis and Christo-genesis, and the fullness of life to come in the *eschaton*, which are instances of wholes encircling each other. These circles spread out from the Eucharist to the worshipping community, to the community of creation and, ultimately, the universe.

Another way in which the Eucharist is related to the *cosmos* is the cycle of life, death and rebirth that is built into the story of the *cosmos*. Within the hidden history of the *cosmos* there is an ongoing process of life and death and the emergence of new life, reaching across billions of years, which includes the stars, galaxies, planets, earth and the community of creation. This process is particularly evident in biological evolution which entails life, followed by vast amounts of death, which, in turn, issues at great cost to effect the emergence of new life. This process is itself a kind of cosmic liturgy. It is here that Eliade's reference to the Christological drama takes on particular significance. The Christological drama is sensed in the observation, by Jesus, that unless the grain of wheat dies, it remains alone, but if it dies, it yields much fruit (John 12:24). This vision of Jesus is also captured in sayings attributed to him about losing one's life to save it (Mark 8:35; Luke 17:30; Matthew 10:39; John 12:25). This teaching of Jesus has dramatic expression in his death on the cross, which is interpreted in a variety of images, such as resurrection, exaltation, glorification and the fullness of life in the Spirit. In this way, the sacrament of the Eucharist celebrates the miraculous dying and rising that took place in the unfolding cosmos and continues to take place in the biological evolution of life on earth and the very recent appearance of human beings.

This pattern of life, death and new life is 'written into the very heart and essence of material creation'.[20] It is a vital part of the life-generating character of nature. It is also, according to Margaret Daly Denton, an insight that can be found in Israel's wisdom tradition.[21] This insight into the nature of creation is also at the centre of Christology: in the historical life, death and resurrection of Jesus as the Christ, and in the teaching of Paul about the seed dying and coming to new life (1 Corinthians 15:36–37). This dynamic pattern of life and death is also represented sacramentally in the breaking of the bread and the pouring of the wine in the celebration of the Eucharist. In this way the Eucharist is connected to the inner life of creation and the historical reality of the Christ-event. This pattern of life and death is often referred to as the Paschal Mystery of Christ, which is at the centre of Christian faith.

A further link in the relationship between Eucharist and cosmos can be found in the ingredients of the Eucharist, which are 'fruit of the earth and work of human hands'. The host of the Eucharist is made up of the raw elements of creation. Bread and wine come from the earth. Through a complex process, different transformations occur. The bread comes from seeds sown in the earth which die to give forth grain, the grain is transformed by humans into bread and the consecrated bread is transformed into the Body of Christ. A similar pattern occurs with the wine: the vine is transformed into grapes and the grapes are crushed into wine which is changed into the Blood of Christ. These transformations take place through the creative action of the Spirit who was present 'in the beginning' and who is continually present in holding creation together and is uniquely active through the invocation of the same creative Spirit in every celebration of the Eucharist. This theology of the Eucharist finds the spirit working at all stages, not just in and through the consecration.

Back to Integral Ecology

This book began with an outline of the teaching of *Laudato Si'* on integral ecology. It sought to sketch some of the implications of the turn to integral ecology for our understanding of theological anthropology, pneumatology, Christology, eschatology and liturgy. It is appropriate to conclude with some reflections on the demands that integral ecology makes on the discourse of *Laudato Si'* on cosmic Eucharist, as outlined above.

Many commentators emphasise the urgency of relating the scientific narratives of the universe to the praxis of faith and theology. A significant voice in this regard is John F. Haught, who has pointed out that

> The intellectual credibility – even the survival – of all religious traditions depends now on how convincingly they adapt their beliefs and aspirations to a scientifically understood universe whose spatial extension, temporal scale, and creative unfolding were unknown to religion's founders and main teachers.[22]

Another commentator who has addressed this new challenge is Jesuit Robert Daly, who is concerned about the language of Eucharistic prayers. Daly asks:

> Is it possible to think and therefore pray, in language and concepts with which contemporary science studies the cosmos (some 13.7 billion years old) in which we are an infinitesimally tiny part?[23]

Daly is acutely aware of how difficult it will be pastorally to achieve this. On the one hand, he is conscious of the existence of many who are comfortably praying within the pre-scientific, three-tiered, earth-centred universe. On the other hand, he is equally mindful of a younger generation who feel alienated and uninspired by this framework when it is used in worship. Daly has scripted a draft Eucharistic prayer that takes account of the scientific view of the universe in which we live.[24] He has subjected his work to the ongoing seminar of the North American Academy of Liturgy on 'Eucharistic Prayers and Theology'. He has also been self-critical of his own attempt at a new Eucharistic prayer and is deeply conscious of the pastoral and liturgical challenges that this entails.

A report on this debate in the *National Catholic Reporter* by Thomas Reese articulates the challenge clearly:

> One of the greatest liturgical challenges of the Church in the 21st century is to figure out how to do liturgy in a way that is meaningful to people in a post-Darwin, post-Einstein, post-Hubble world.[25]

Reese is concerned that current 'liturgical worship requires that we park our scientific minds at the church door and enter into the pre-scientific world of our ancestors when we pray'.

There is no easy answer to this pressing liturgical and pastoral leap of imagination. Some are hesitant about linking the Eucharistic prayer to a theory of science that will change over time. Others argue for some relationship to the culture of science if the Eucharistic prayer is to make sense to a generation that takes the evolutionary story for granted. It must be acknowledged that the mindset of *Laudato Si'* and, in particular, the teaching of the encyclical on the cosmic Eucharist, opens up new possibilities in this debate.

In addition, the full weight of *Veritatis Gaudium* (2018) and the Naples address of Pope Francis on theology on 21 June 2019, both summarised in Chapter 1, ought to be brought to bear on this dialogue between liturgy and the culture of science, between a focus on the cosmic Eucharist in *Laudato Si'* and our contemporary understanding of the universe in which we live. As seen in Chapter 1, these documents call for a 'radical paradigm shift', a 'bold cultural revolution', the adaptation of faith to various cultures, and a recognition that we are now living in an era of multiple crises: anthropological, environmental, ethical, spiritual and theological. In addition, Pope Francis says that the renewal of theology will succeed 'only if it is done with an open mind and on one's knees'.

To open this debate, and that is all that can be done here, it is necessary to say what this dialogue between liturgy and cosmology entails and does not entail. It is not about replacing the Eucharistic narrative with one or other of the new cosmic stories; it is not about conflating faith with culture or reducing liturgical faith to fashion; it is not about abandoning the historically established Eucharistic narrative of the New Testament. Instead, it is about *reframing* the context in which the established Eucharistic narrative is proclaimed; it is about taking account of the age, size and dynamism of the evolving universe in which the Eucharistic narrative is prayed; it is, to use the language of Charles Taylor, about changing the 'cosmic imaginary' from being static and earth-centred to being dynamic and evolutionary. These shifts should not be seen as threats to faith and liturgy, but as enhancements of the practices of worship. If the framing in which prayer and liturgy takes place is out of sympathy or, in some cases, in conflict with, the established truths of science, it is difficult to foresee a future for inspiring, meaningful and spiritually engaging Christian celebrations of the Eucharist. It is the view of this chapter that *Laudato Si'*, *Veritatis Gaudium* (28 January 2018) and the Naples address of Pope Francis (21 June 2019) have opened the way for a more serious and imaginative engagement between liturgy and science, and between cosmic Eucharist and cosmic stories.

A further starting point for this dialogue would be to look at the existing Prefaces and Eucharistic prayers. Louvain liturgist Joris Geldhof has examined the Prefaces and the Eucharistic prayers of the *Ordo Missae*.[26] His findings are pertinent to this particular debate. After a careful examination of the content of the Prefaces and Eucharistic prayers, he concludes that: 'Creation is by no means a dominant theme in the fifty Prefaces of the *Ordo Missae*. The Incarnation and its many effects are much more dominant'.[27] Similarly, after examining the four main Eucharistic prayers, he concludes that: 'Creation is not a dominant topic in any of the four Eucharistic-prayers'.[28]

To be more specific, the fifth Preface of the eight Prefaces for Sundays in Ordinary Time is entitled 'Creation' and is, therefore, of interest to the question we are exploring here. Geldhof notes that the fifth Preface talks about God the Father laying 'the foundations of the world', arranging 'the changing of times and seasons', forming 'man in your own image', and setting 'humanity over the whole world … to rule in your name over all you have made'. Geldhof, sensitive to the ambiguity here, says: 'To take this Preface as justification of the violence humanity is exerting on the earth … would not do justice to the text as a whole'.[29] There is, however, in spite of Geldhof's understandable defence of this Preface, an ambiguity surrounding the concept of humanity ruling. As seen in Chapter 6 on, ruling and having dominion have, over the centuries, slipped into a model of domination that has been used to legitimise the exploitation of the earth's resources. Further, as we have seen in that same chapter, one way of overcoming this is to move towards the adoption of a community of creation model.

The third and fourth Eucharistic prayers, in contrast to the first and second, reflect a more developed understanding of creation. The third Eucharistic prayer acknowledges God as creator in a doxological way. It also affirms that God, through the Son and the Spirit, vivifies and sanctifies everything.

The fourth Eucharistic prayer is regarded by many as the most creation-centred of all of the four Eucharistic prayers. It begins with creation, has many biblical allusions within it, and generally it adopts a positive attitude to the world and has several inspiring verses on the role of the Spirit. However, in the midst of these positive features, it does say: 'You formed man in your own image and entrusted the whole world to his care, so that in serving you alone, the Creator, he might have dominion over all creatures.'

To be fair to these Eucharistic prayers, the idea of humanity's rule and dominion over all creatures does, in truth, reflect the original meaning of dominion, namely the human acting as a representative of the king and doing, therefore, as the king would wish for the well-being of his subjects. However, as seen in Chapter 6, the reception of dominion has slipped into domination, and has been used as a justification for the exploitation of nature and the earth's resources. Whether dominion can be rescued in the twenty-first century is the subject of some debate. Further, account should be taken of the correction called for by *Laudato Si'* concerning the misunderstanding of this particular interpretation of Genesis. In commenting on these Eucharistic prayers, and especially the examples taken, one cannot ignore or gloss over, in silence, the sexist language in use within the

Eucharistic prayers for which there is no excuse today. These glaring problems of sexist language and discrimination must be included in the dialogue between liturgy and culture today.

Before concluding this short section on integral ecology and the cosmic Eucharist, it should be noted that there are a number of significant advantages attached to the possibility of incorporating some perspectives from the different cosmologies into the context in which we worship and the ways in which we worship. In doing this, there would be a pastoral outreach to those who feel alienated by the existing celebrations of the Eucharist. Further, the credibility of Eucharistic celebrations would be enhanced by reframing the context in a way that recognises some aspects of the scientific understanding of the world in which we live. By allowing science to influence the context of Christian worship, one would also be implementing the vision of *Laudato Si'* and its particular emphasis on the cosmic Eucharist. Furthermore, in doing this, the liturgy would be following through on the logic of integral ecology as outlined in Chapter 1 of this book. And, lastly, it should be noted that the mind of the Second Vatican Council on the reform of the liturgy proposes that:

> It is the wish of the Church that all the faithful should be led to take full, conscious and active participation in liturgical celebrations.[30]

This particular principle from the council has far-reaching consequences: it embraces issues around liturgy and integral ecology, the relationship between the cosmic Eucharist and the contemporary understanding of living in an evolutionary universe, and serious issues surrounding the sexist language within the liturgy. In seeking a balance between liturgy and cosmology, one is reminded of the remark by Holmes Rolston III:

> Religion married to science will be a widow tomorrow. But religion divorced from science will leave no offspring.[31]

To conclude, the last two chapters, which are closely related, the vision and flow of ideas can be represented in this diagram:

Creation
↓
Throne of God
↓
Worship in the Jewish Temple
↓
The Ambiguity of Dominion
↓
The Community of Creation Model
↓
Theological Bridges to the Natural World
↓
Nature as a Sacrament of Communion
↓
Challenges posed by Eliade
↓
Laudato Si' on Eucharist
↓
John Paul II and Benedict XVI
↓
The Influence of Teilhard de Chardin
↓
The Cosmic Eucharist
↓
Prefaces and Eucharistic Prayers

Perhaps the best summary can be found in the words of Elizabeth Barrett Browning (1806–1861):

Earth's crammed with heaven,
and every common bush afire with God,
but only he who sees takes off his shoes;
the rest sit round and pluck blackberries.[32]

Endnotes

Foreword

1   Gregory Dix, *The State of the Liturgy,* London: Dacre Press, Adam and Charles Black, 1945, p.157.

Endnotes Chapter 1

1   *Laudato Si': On Care of our Common Home*, 2015, a. 3. Hereafter the encyclical will be referred to as *LS* and references to it will appear in the body of the text as, for example *LS*, 3.
2   See Austin Ivereigh, 'Why call it Progress?', *Commonweal,* October 2019: 46–53, at 52–53.
3   Seán McDonagh, '*Laudato Si'*: A Prophetic challenge for the 21st century', in *Laudato Si', An Irish Response: Essays on the Pope's Letter on the Environment*, edited by Seán McDonagh, Dublin: Veritas Publications 2017, 7–29.
4   See Anthony Kelly, *Laudato Si': An Integral Ecology and the Catholic Vision*, Australia: ATF Press, 2016: 1.
5   Elizabeth Johnson at Fordham Prep (School) in the Bronx on Laetare Sunday, March 2016, as a member of a panel discussion.
6   Reinhard Cardinal Marx, "Everything is Connected": On the Relevance of an Integral Understanding of Reality in Laudato Si', in *Theological Studies,* June 2016: 295–307, at 295.
7   Ibid.
8   Denis Edwards, 'Introduction', in *The Christian Understanding of Creation: A Historical Trajectory*, Minneapolis, MN: Fortress Press, 2017: xi.
9   This sketchy potted history, and selected quotations, is indebted to Sam Mickey, Sean Kelly and Adam Robert, 'Introduction: The History and Future of Integral Ecologies', in *The Variety of Integral Ecologies: Nature, Culture, and Knowledge in the Planetary Era*, Sam Mickey, Sean Kelly and Adam Robert (eds.), New York, NY: SUNY Press, 2017: 1–27.
10 As cited by Sam Mickey, Sean Kelly and Adam Robert, ibid., 14.
11 Sean Kelly, 'Five Principles of Integral Ecology', in *The Variety of Integral Ecologies*, op. cit., 189–227.
12 Ibid., 193. A similar and equally persuasive critique of modern culture and science can be found in *The New Cosmic Story: Inside our Awakening Universe*, by John F. Haught, New Haven, CT: Yale University Press, 2017.
13 https://www.bbc.com/news/business-50868717. Accessed 15 February 2020.
14 A sharper and more detailed critique, with extensive references to experts associated with the Report can be found in Daniel P. Castillo, 'Integral Ecology as a Liberationist Concept', in *Theological Studies,* June 2016: 353–76, and Daniel P. Castillo, 'Against the Unity of Babel: Liberation Theology and the Language of Sustainable Development', in *Theology and Ecology across the Disciplines: On the Care for our Common Home*, edited by Celia Deane-Drummond and Rebecca Artinian-Kaiser, New York, NY: T & T Clarke, 2018: 119–131.
15 Post-Synodal Apostolic Exhortation, *Querida Amazonia*, a. 58.
16 Denis Edwards, 'Sublime Communion: The Theology of the Natural World', *Theological Studies*, June 2016: 377–91, at 378.
17 Celia Deane-Drummond, '*Laudato Si'* and the Natural Sciences: An Assessment of Possibilities and Limits', in *Theological Studies,* June 2016: 392–415, at 403. McDonagh emphasises that the loss of biodiversity 'has enormous implications for Christian living in our world today', Seán McDonagh, art. cit., 24.
18 Elizabeth A. Johnson, *Creation and the Cross: The Mercy of God for a Planet in Peril*, New York, NY: Orbis Books, 2018: 226.
19 Seán McDonagh, art. cit., 24.
20 *Veritatis Gaudium*, a. 1.
21 Ibid., a.3.
22 Ibid., a.3.
23 Ibid., a.3.
24 Ibid., a.3.

25 Ibid., a.4, a).
26 Ibid., a.4, b).
27 Ibid., a.4, c).
28 Ibid., a.4, d).
29 Ibid., *Norms*, a.3, no. 1.
30 See *Gaudium et Spes*, a.40–45; 62.
31 *Gaudium et Spes*, a.40–45. See commentary on *Gaudium et Spes*, with particular reference to the principle of mutuality in relation to the dialogue between the Church and the world in Dermot Lane, 'Keeping the Memory Alive: Vatican II as an enduring Legacy for the Reform of the Church', in *Vatican II in Ireland: Fifty Years On*, edited by Dermot A. Lane, New York, NY: Peter Lang, 2015: 29–53, at 42–44.
32 'Message of His Holiness Pope John Paul II', *Physics, Philosophy and Theology: A Common Quest for Understanding*, edited by Robert J. Russell, William R. Stoeger, SJ, and George V. Coyne, SJ, Vatican Observatory/University of Notre Dame Press, 1988: at m11.
33 Ibid., 13.
34 22 October 1996.
35 See Genesis 1–2:7 and Romans 5:5.
36 1 John 4: 8, 16.
37 Remarks at an Assembly of the Pontifical Academy of Sciences on 27 October 2014.
38 Denis Edwards, 'Creation seen in the light of Christ: A Theological Sketch', in *The Natural World and God: Theological Explorations*, Australia: AFT, 2017: 3–21, at 12.

Endnotes Chapter 2

1   Available online as 'Subjective well-being over the life course', London School of Economics, 12–13 December 2016. Last accessed on 16 March 2020.
2   Rowan Williams, *Being Human: Bodies, Minds, Persons*, London: SPCK, 2018: VII.
3   Lynn White Jr, 'The Historical Roots of our Ecologic Crisis', *Science*, 155, 1967: 1203–07.
4   Video talk by Berry at Schumacher College, USA, available online at www.thomasberry.org and subsequently published as 'Reinventing the Human', in Thomas Berry, *The Great Work: Our Way into the Future*, New York, NY: Harmony/Bell Tower, 199: 159ff.
5   Elizabeth Johnson, *Ask the Beasts: Darwin and the God of Love*, New York, NY: Bloomsbury, 2014: 2.
6   Dan Horan, 'Deconstructing Anthropocentric Privilege: *Imago Dei* and Non-Human Agency', in *The Heythrop Journal*, 60, 2019: 560–70, at 560–61.
7   David G. Kirchhoffer, 'How Ecology can save the Life of Theology: A Philosophical Contribution to the Engagement of Ecology and Theology', in *Theology and Ecology across the Disciplines: On Care for our Common Home*, edited by Celia Deane-Drummond and Rebecca Artinian-Kaiser, London: T & T Clarke, 2018: 53–63, at 57.
8   Neil Ormerod and Christina Vanin, 'Ecological Conversion: What does it mean?', in *Theological Studies*, Volume 77 (2), 2016: 328–52 at 341–2.
9   Charles Taylor, *A Secular Age*, Cambridge, MA: Harvard University Press, 2007, 363.
10 Richard Rorty, *Consequences of Pragmatism*, Minnesota, University of Minnesota, 1982: xliii.
11 Michel Foucault, *The Order of things: An Archaeology of the Human Sciences*, New York, NY: Random House, 1970, 387.
12 See Ormerod and Vanin, op. cit., 341.
13 See Elizabeth A. Johnson, *Woman, Earth and Creator Spirit*, 1993 Madeleva Lecture in Spirituality, New York: Paulist Press, 1993; and Mary Doak, 'Sex, Race and Culture: Constructing Theological Anthropology for the 21st Century', in *Theological Studies*, volume 80 (3), 2019: 508–29; and Ann Clifford, 'Pope Francis's *Laudato Si*', On Care for our Common Home: An Eco-Feminist Response', CTSA Proceedings, 72–2017. Heather Eaton questions the patriarchal, hierarchical dualistic world view of Genesis 1 and 2, pointing out that 'domination of earth is enmeshed with the oppression of women'; details in Hilary Marlow, 'What Am I in a Boundless Creation', in *Biblical*, 2014.
14 Arthur Peacocke, 'Theology and Science Today', in *Cosmos as Creation*, edited by Ted Peters, Nashville, TN: Abington Press, 1989: 32.
15 Stephen Hawking, *A Brief History of Time*, New York, NY: Bantam Books, 1988: 121–122.

16 Pierre Teilhard de Chardin SJ, *The Human Phenomenon,* translated by Sarah Appleton-Webber, Eastbourne: Sussex Academic Press, 1999: 56.

17 P. Teilhard de Chardin SJ, *Human Energy,* London: Collins, 1966, 57–58.

18 Thomas Berry, *Evening Thoughts: Reflecting on the Earth as a Sacred community,* San Francisco, CA: Sierra Club, 2006, 17–18.

19 Lieve Orye, 'Being Human, Doing Research in a World of Systemic Injustice: Reflections on Alina Hankela's Liberationist Ethnography', in *Louvain Studies,* Fall 2018: 249–68, at 250–53.

20 This understanding of the natural world has been developed in much greater depth and detail by the scientist William Stoeger SJ in various places such as 'The Mind – Brain Problem: Laws of Nature and Constitutive Relationships', in *Neuroscience and the Person: Scientific Perspectives and Divine Action,* edited by Robert J. Russell et al., Vatican City: Vatican Observatory; Berkeley, CA, 1999: 129–46. Denis Edwards has developed, to good effect, Stoeger's thesis about the constitutive character of relationships among humans and within the natural world in a number of places, such as 'Towards a Theology of Divine Action: W. R. Stoeger, SJ on the Laws of Nature', in *The Natural World and God: Theological Explorations,* Australia: AFT Publishing Group, 2017: 269–91; and 'Ecological Theology: Trinitarian Perspectives', in *CTSA Proceedings,* 72, 2017: 14–28.

21 *The Pastoral Constitution on the Church in the Modern World,* 1965, a. 22.

22 Ibid., a. 24.

23 One of the most persuasive retrievals of the *kenosis* model of self-emptying is to be found in Sarah Coakley's article on '*Kenosis* and Subversion' in *Powers and Submissions: Spirituality, Philosophy and Gender,* Oxford: Wiley & Sons, 2009: 4–49. In this article, Coakley takes the example of self-surrender that takes place in contemplative prayer. She writes: 'Only, I suggest, by facing – and giving new expression to – the paradoxes of 'losing one's life in order to save it' can feminists hope to construct a vision of the Christic self that transcends gender stereotypes we are seeking to up-end', ibid. 33.

24 See Sarah Coakley, *God, Sexuality, and the Self,* Cambridge: Cambridge University Press, 2013: 56–8 and 318.

25 Catherine M. LaCugna, *God for Us: The Trinity and Christian Life,* New York, NY: HarperSanFrancisco, 1991: 14, 15.

26 Declan Marmion and Rick Van Nieuwenhove, *An Introduction to the Trinity,* Cambridge: Cambridge University Press, 2011: 205. It should be noted that Marmion and Van Nieuwenhove are quoting Douglas H. Knight, editor, *Theology of John Zizioulas: Personhood and the Church,* Eldershot: Ashgate, 2007: 2.

27 Ibid., 205.

28 Marmion and Van Nieuwenhove make this point in a footnote with reference to John Polkinghorne, *Science and Theology: The Christian Encounter with Reality,* London: SPCK, 2004: 74–75.

Endnotes Chapter 3

1 Charles Taylor, *Sources of the Self: The Making of Modern Identity,* Cambridge: Cambridge University Press, 1989: 520.

2 Mark Wallace, 'The Wounded Spirit as basis for Hope in an Age of Radical Ecology', in *Christianity and Ecology: Seeking the Well-Being of Earth and Humans,* edited by D.T. Hessel and Rosemary R. Ruether Cambridge, MA: Harvard University Press, 2000: 5–72, at 55.

3 Daniel Castelo, *Pneumatology: A Guide for the Perplexed,* London: Bloomsbury, 2015: 74–75.

4 *Laudato Si'* dedicates Chapter Six to 'Ecological Education and Spirituality'.

5 John R. Levison, *The Jewish Origin of Christian Pneumatology,* The Duquesne University 11th Annual Holy Spirit Lecture, 2017: 8.

6 Daniel Castelo, op. cit., 29 and 67; Erin Lothes Biviano, 'Elizabeth Johnson and Cantors of the Universe: The Indwelling Renewing and Moving Creator Spirit and a Pneumatology from Below', in *Turning to the Heavens and the Earth: Theological Reflections on a Cosmological Conversion, Essays in Honour of Elizabeth A. Johnson,* edited by Julia Brumbaugh and Natalia Imperatori-Lee, Collegeville, MN: Liturgical Press, 2016: 174–95.

7 T. S. Eliot, 'Four Quartets, Dry Salvages', in *The Complete Poems and Plays of T. S. Eliot,* London: Faber & Faber, 1969, 18.

8 Seamus Heaney, 'Postscript', in *The Spirit Level,* London: Faber & Faber, 1996, 70.

9   Denis O'Driscoll, *Stepping Stones, Interviews with Seamus Heaney*, London: Faber & Faber, 2008: 366.

10   Seamus Heaney, 'St Kevin and the Blackbird', in *The Spirit Level*, op. cit., 20–21.

11   J. C. Eccles, *Brain and Conscious Experience*, Berlin: Springer Verlag, 1962: 327.

12   These three examples are informed in part by E. A. Johnson and Erin Lothes Biviano's article referenced in footnote 6.

13   Gerard Manley Hopkins, 'God's Grandeur', in *The Poetical Works of Gerard Manley Hopkins*, edited by Norman H. MacKenzie, Oxford: Clarendon, 1990, 111.

14   'Lines composed a few miles above Tintern Abbey, on revisiting the banks of the Wye during a tour', 13 July 1798, by William Wordsworth (1770–1850). For this reading of Wordsworth I am influenced by Brian Cosgrove, 'A Dualistic Theophany: Nature as Source of Fear and Love in Wordsworth', in *Performing the Word: Festschrift for Ronan Drury*, edited by Enda McDonagh, Dublin: Columba Press, 2014: 170–77, at 171–72.

15   Catherine de Vinck, *Gifting*, The Forum on Religion and Ecology at Yale, online *Newsletter*, May 2019, accessed 24 March 2020.

16   Stephen Hawking, *A Brief History of Time*, New York, NY: Bantam Books, 1988: 174.

17   Details available in Andrew R. Davis, 'Spirit, Wind or Breath: Reflections on the Old Testament', in *The Holy Spirit: Setting the World on Fire*, Richard Lennan and Nancy Pineda-Madrid, Mahwah, NJ: Paulist Press, 2017,9, for reference to Edwards.

18   These images are influenced by different translations of Genesis 1 which in turn are shaped by Deuteronomy 32:11.

19   J.R. Levison, *The Jewish Origin of Christian Pneumatology*, Holy Spirit Lecture, Duquesne University, 2017: 5.

20   Andrew R. Davis, op. cit., 63–72.

21   Theodore Hiebert, 'Air, the First Sacred Thing: Conception of *Ruach* in the Hebrew Scriptures', in Denis Edwards, *Breath of Life: A Theology of the Creator Spirit*, New York, NY: Orbis Books, 2004: 107.

22   Amos Yong, 'Beginning with the Spirit: Biblical Motifs for a Foundational Pneumatology', *Spirit-Word-Community: Theological Hermeneutics in Trinitarian Perspective*, Farnham: Ashgate Publishing, 2002: 27–48, at 43–47.

23   Erin Lothes Biviano, art cit.,183.

24   Karl Rahner SJ, *The Mystical in Everyday Life: Sermons, Essays and Prayers,* , edited by Annemarie Kidder, New York, NY: Orbis Books, 2010: 52–58.

25   T. Hiebert, op. cit., 10 and 17–18.

26   Haight, Roger, 'Spirituality, Evolution, Creator God', in *Theological Studies,* June 2018: 251–73, at 253,

27   'The Spiritual Power of Matter', *Hymn of the Universe*, London: Collins, 1965: 59–71.

28   *Hymn of the Universe*, London: Collins, 1965: 68–71.

29   Pierre Teilhard de Chardin SJ, *The Heart of Matter,* San Diego, CA: Harcourt, 1978: 35.

30   See Kathleen Duffy, *Teilhard's Struggle: Embracing the Work of Evolution*, New York, NY: Orbis Books, 2019: 2.

31   *Human Energy*, London: Collins, 1969: 57–58.

32   *The Human Phenomenon*, Oregon: Sussex Academic Press, 1999: 6.

33   John Feehan, *The Dipper's Acclaim and Other Essays*, Dalgan Park, Columban Ecological Institute, 2016: 82.

34   Janet M. Soskice, '*Creatio ex Nihilo*: Jewish and Christian Foundations', in *Creation and the God of Abraham*, edited by David Burrell, Carlo Cogliati, Janet M. Soskice and William Stoeger, Cambridge: Cambridge University Press, 2010: 39.

35   Karl Rahner, 'The Unity of Spirit and Matter in Christian Understanding', in *Theological Investigations,* Vol. VI: 153–77.

36   Ibid, 169.

37   This claim does not preclude the possibility that the universe is becoming conscious of itself in other places, such as extra-terrestrial ones.

38   Karl Rahner, 'Natural Science and Reasonable Faith', in *Theological Investigations,* Vol. XXI, 1985: 16–55.

39   Karl Rahner, 'Festival of the Future of the World', in *Theological Investigations,* Vol. VII: 183.

40   Ibid., 184.

41 John Damascene, 'First Apology against those who attack Divine Images', par. 16, *On Divine Image: Three Apologies Against Those Who Attack Divine Images*, translated by David Andersen, Yonkers, NY: St Vladimir's Seminary Press, 1980, par. 16.

42 Ilia Delio, 'Revisiting the Franciscan Doctrine of Christ', in *Theological Studies*, March 2003: 3–24, at 13.

43 An introduction to this aspect of Bonaventure's theology can be found in Ilia Delio, *A Franciscan View of Creation: Learning to Live in a Sacramental World*, Ashland, OH: Bookmasters, 2003.

44 I am grateful to Terry Tilley for bringing this point to my attention.

Endnotes Chapter 4

1 Gregersen developed the concept of deep Incarnation in the context of an evolutionary Christianity in an article entitled 'The Cross of Christ in an Evolutionary World', in *Dialog: A Journal of Theology*, 40: 2 (2001): 192–207. Since then Gregersen has, in a variety of articles, applied the concept of deep Incarnation to the whole of Christology. An extensive analysis of deep Incarnation and its application to Christology can be found in *Incarnation: On the Scope and Depth of Christology*, edited by Niels Henrik Gregersen, Minneapolis, MN: Fortress Press, 2015.

2 Karl Rahner, *Foundations of Christian Faith: An Introduction to the Idea of Christianity*, London: Darton, Longman & Todd, 1978, 197.

3 Karl Rahner, 'Christology Today', *Theological Investigations*, Vol. XXI, 220–27, London: Darton, Longman & Todd, 220–227, at 227.

4 On the meaning and value of a low-ascending Christology see Dermot Lane, *The Reality of Jesus: An Essay in Christology*, Dublin: Veritas Publications, 1975; and *Stepping Stones to Other Religions*, Dublin: Veritas Publications, 2011: 277.

5 This scheme of Exodus 1–3 is taken from Richard Clifford. See podcast by Richard Clifford at bc.edu/encore, 'The Old Testament in the Christian Bible', accessed 23 July 2019.

6 I am indebted here to the helpful article by Gerald O'Collins on 'Word, Spirit, and Wisdom in the Universe: A Biblical and Theological Reflection', in *Incarnation: On the Scope and Depth of Christology*, edited by Niels H. Gregersen, Minneapolis, MN: Fortress Press, 2015: 59–77.

7 Martin Hengel as quoted by Nils Henrik Gregersen in 'Christology', in *Systematic Theology and Climate Change: Ecumenical Perspectives*, edited by Michael S. Northcott and Peter M. Scott, Oxford: Routledge, 2014: 43. Gregersen is quoting from an article by Hengel in German, 'Jesus als messianischer Lehrer der Weisheit und die Anfaenge der Christologie', in *Sagesse et religion. Colloque de Strasbourg*, Paris: Presses Universitaires de France, 1979: 304–44.

8 James C. Dunn, *Christology in the Making: A New Testament Enquiry into the Origins of the Doctrine of the Incarnation*, Philadelphia, PA: Westminster, 1980: 212.

9 Raymond Brown, *The Gospel according to John*, 1–xvii, New York, NY: Doubleday, 1966: CXXII.

10 Ibid., CXXIII–CXXIV.

11 Elizabeth A. Johnson, *Creation and the Cross: The Mercy of God for a Planet in Peril*, New York, NY: Orbis Books, 2018: 170 and 177.

12 Erin Lothes Biviano, 'Elizabeth A. Johnson and Cantors of the Universe: The Indwelling, Renewing, and Moving Creator Spirit and a Pneumatology from below', in *Turning to the heavens and the earth: Theological Reflections on a Cosmological Conversion, Essay in Honour of Elizabeth A. Johnson*, edited by Julia Bumbaugh and Nattali Imperatori, Collegeville, MN: Liturgical Press, 2016, 182.

13 Arne Næss and D. Rathenberg, *Ecology, Community and Lifestyle: Outline of an Ecosophy*, Cambridge, UK: Cambridge University Press, 1989: 29. See also Sam Michey, Sean Kelly and Adam Robbert (eds.), 'Introduction', *A Variety of Integral Ecologies: Nature, Culture and Knowledge in a Planetary Era*, New York, NY: SUNY, 2017: 6–7.

14 Nils H. Gregersen, 'The Extended Body of Christ: Three Dimensions of Deep Incarnation', in *Incarnation: On the Scope and Depth of Eschatology*, op. cit., 225–51, at 225–26.

15 Nils H. Gregersen, 'A Cross of Christ in an Evolutionary World', in *Dialog: A Journal of Theology, 40, 2*, 2001: 192–207. See also N. H. Gregersen, 'Christology', in *Systematic Theology and Climate Change: Ecumenical Perspectives*, edited by Michael Northcoff and Peter M. Scott, London: Routledge, 2014.

16 Edward Schillebeeckx, *Interim Report on the Books, Jesus and Christ*, London: SCM Press, 1980: 126–27.

17 Richard Bauckham, 'The Incarnation and the Cosmic Christ', in *Incarnation: On the Scope and Depth of Christology*, ed. by Niels Gregersen, Minneapolis, MN: Fortress Press, 2015: 25–56, at 37–45.

18 E. A. Johnson, 'Jesus and the Cosmos: Soundings in Deep Christology', in *Incarnation: On the Scope and Depth of Christology*, op. cit., 134.

19 E. A. Johnson, 'Jesus and the Cosmos', op. cit., 151.

20 Nils H. Gregersen, 'The Extended Body of Christ', op, cit., 225–51, at 233.

21 Ibid., 242.

22 Holmes Rolston III, 'Divine Presence – Causal, Cybernetic, Caring, Cruciform: From Information to Incarnation', in *Incarnation: On the Scope and Depth of Christology*, op. cit., 255–87, at 264.

23 Nils H. Gregersen, *Incarnation*, op. cit., 325.

24 I am indebted to Terrence Tilley for bringing this point to my attention.

25 Karl Rahner, *Foundations of Christian Faith*, op. cit.,197.

Endnotes Chapter 5

1 J. B. Metz, 'Theology Today: New Crises and New Visions', in *Proceedings of the Catholic Theological Society of America*, 40, 1985: 13.

2 David Bentley Hart, 'The Devil's March: '*Creatio ex nihilo*, The Problem of Evil, and a Few Dostoyevskian Meditations', in *Creation* ex nihilo*: Origins, Development, Contemporary Challenges*, edited by Gary A. Anderson and Markus Bockmuehl, Notre Dame, IN: University of Notre Dame Press, 2018: 297–318, at 303.

3 See John Haught, 'The Unfinished Universe: Is God at Work?', in *Commonweal*, 14 March 2003: 12–14, and also his book *The Cosmic Story: Inside our Awakening Universe*, New Haven, CT: Yale University Press, 2017.

4 David Bentley Hart, art. cit., 303.

5 See Mark D. Owens, *As it was in the Beginning: An Intertextual Analysis of the New Creation in Galatians, Second Corinthians and Ephesians*, Eugene, OR: Pickwick, 2015.

6 This commentary is indebted, in part, to Dianne Bergent, *A New Heaven, A New Earth*, New York, NY: Orbis Books, 2016: 151–59.

7 See *Louvain Studies*, 40, 2017: 36–57.

8 The term 'agent' is used by Anthony Thiselton in *The Holy Spirit: In Biblical Teaching, through the Centuries and Today*, London: SPCK, 2013: 82 and 194.

9 Brendan Byrne, *Romans*, Sacra Pagina 6, Collegeville, MN: Liturgical Press, 1996: 255.

10 See the pioneering article by Peter Phan, 'Eschatology and Ecology: The Environment in the End-Time', in *ITQ*, vol. 62, 1996/1997: 3–16.

11 The same the footnote, number 53, refers to the use of Teilhard by Popes Paul VI, John Paul II and Benedict XVI.

12 Nathan W. O'Halloran deals with these questions in greater detail in '"Each creature, resplendently transfigured": Development of Teaching in *Laudato Si'*, in *Theological Studies*, 2018, vol. 79 (2): 376–98, especially 396.

13 Denis Edwards, 'Resurrection and the Costs of Evolution: A Dialogue with Rahner on Non-Interventionist Theology', in *The Natural World and God: Theological Explorations*, Australia: AFT Publishing, 2017: 295–316, at 304.

14 Elizabeth A. Johnson, *Creation and the Cross: The Mercy of God for a Planet in Peril*, New York, NY: Orbis Books, 2018: 100.

15 Karl Rahner, 'Resurrection: D. Theology', in *Encyclopaedia of Theology: A Concise Sacramentum Mundi*, edited by K. Rahner, London: Burns & Oates, 1975: 1442.

16 Ibid.

17 Ibid., 1142.

18 Karl Rahner, 'Jesus' Resurrection', in *Theological Investigations*, Vol. 17, London: Darton, Longman & Todd,16–23, at 22.

19 Karl Rahner, 'A Faith that Loves the Earth', in *The Great Church Year: The Best of Karl Rahner's*

Homiles, Sermons, and Meditations, edited by A. Raff and H. Egan, New York, NY: Crossroad, 1994,195.

20 Denis Edwards, *How God Acts: Creation, Redemption and Special Divine Action,* Minneapolis, MN: Fortress Press, 2010: 105.

21 *GS,* 39.

22 Karl Rahner, 'Hidden Victory', *Theological Investigations,* Vol. 7, London: Darton, Longman & Todd,151–58, at 156.

23 Karl Rahner, 'The Question of the Future', in *Theological Investigations,* Vol. 12, London: Darton, Longman & Todd, 181–201, at 181 and 198.

24 Paul Ricoeur, 'Hope and the Structure of Philosophical Systems', in *Proceedings of the American Catholic Philosophical Association:* 1970: 55–69.

Endnotes Chapter 6

1   Some of these questions have been addressed by Dermot Lane in 'Eucharistie et Justice Sociale', Congrès Eucharistique Lourdes 1981, in *Eucharistie: Vers un Monde Nouveau,* Paris: Editions du Centurion, 1981: 203–13, and in 'Eucharist as Sacrament of the Eschaton: A Failure of the Imagination' in *50th International Eucharistic Congress: Proceedings of the International Symposium of Theology: The Ecclesiology of Communion Fifty Years after the Opening of Vatican II,* Vol. 3, Dublin: Veritas Publications, 2013: 399–414.

2   Charles Taylor, 'Western Secularity', in *Rethinking Secularism,* edited by Craig Calhoun, M. Juergensmeyer and J. Van Antwerpen, New York, NY: Oxford University Press, 2011: 38.

3   See William P. Brown, *The Seven Pillars of Creation: Bible, Science, and Ecology,* New York, NY: Oxford University Press, 2010: 6.

4   Ibid., 36.

5   William P. Brown, op. cit., 37.

6   Terence Fretheim, *God and the World of the Old Testament: A Relational Theology of Creation,* Nashville, TN: Abington Press, 2005: 31.

7   Ibid., 31.

8   Ibid., 32.

9   William P. Brown, op. cit., 79.

10 Walter Brueggemann, *Theology of the Old Testament: Testimony, Dispute, Advocacy,* Minneapolis, MN: Fortress Press, 1997: 153.

11 William P. Brown, op. cit., devotes a whole chapter to creation as 'the cosmic temple: cosmogony according to Genesis 1:1–2:3'.

12 Jon Levenson, *Creation and the Persistence of Evil: The Jewish Drama of Divine Omnipotence,* New York, NY: Harper & Row, 1988: 86.

13 Simon Oliver, *Creation: A Guide for the Perplexed,* London: Bloomsbury T & T Clark, 2017: 18.

14 Margaret Barker develops this theme in further detail in *Creation: A Biblical Vision for the Environment,* New York, T & T Clark International, 2010: Chapter 1.

15 Simon Oliver, op. cit., 13, and 161, n. 13. Oliver gives the following quotation from Philo: 'We ought to look upon the universal world as the highest and truest temple of God', taken from *The Works of Philo: Complete and Unabridged,* Peabody: Hendrickson Publishers, 2002: 540.

16 Ann Clifford, 'From Ecological Lament to Sustainable Oikos', in *Environmental Stewardship: Critical Perspectives – Past and Present,* edited by R. J. Berry, London: T & T Clark, 2006: 247–52, at 252.

17 Jürgen Moltmann, *God in Creation: An Ecological Doctrine of Creation,* London: SCM Press Ltd., 1985: 276–96.

18 I am grateful to Terrence Tilley for nuancing the meaning of 'dominion' in the context of liturgy.

19 Denis Edwards, *Christian Understandings of Creation: The Historical Trajectory,* Minneapolis, MN: Fortress Press, 2017: 2–5.

20 Richard Bauckham, *The Bible and Ecology: Rediscovering the Community of Creation,* London: Darton, Longman & Todd, 2010: 2–11.

21 Elizabeth Johnson, *Ask the Beasts: Darwin and the God of Love,* New York, NY: Bloomsbury, 2014: 265–67.

22 Dan P. Horan, *All God's Creatures: A Theology of Creation*, New York, NY: Lexington Books/ Fortress Press, 2018, Part 1.

23 These arguments are developed in greater length and depth by Johnson in *Ask the Beasts*, op. cit., 265–66, and Dan P. Horan in *All God's Creatures*, op. cit., Chapter 3.

24 See Elizabeth A. Johnson, *Women, Earth, and Creator Spirit*, 1993 Madeleva Lecture in Spirituality, Mahwah, NJ: Paulist Press, 1993: 29–40.

25 Alfred Whitehead, *Modes of Thought*, New York, NY: The Free Press, 1968: 110.

26 Alice Walker, *The Color Purple*, New York, NY: Pocket Books, 1982: 178.

27 On the interconnectedness of everything, see: *Laudato Si'*, 16, 42, 70, 91, 117, 137, 138, 141, 142. On inter-relationality, see *Laudato Si'*, 120, 137. On interdependence, see *Laudato Si'*, 164.

28 These complementary ways of expressing the Trinity are developed by Dermot Lane in 'Pneumatological Foundations for a Catholic Theology of Interreligious Dialogue', in *The Past, Present and Future of Theologies of Interreligious Dialogue*, edited by Terrence Merrigan and John Friday, Oxford: Oxford University Press, 2017: 28–46.

29 See Elizabeth A. Johnson, *Ask the Beasts*, op. cit., 267–73 and 281–83. See also Elizabeth A. Johnson, *Creation and the Cross: The Mercy of God for a Planet in Peril*, New York, NY: Orbis Books, 2018: 216–21.

30 See Seán Freyne, 'Jesus and the Ecology of Galilee', in *Jesus, A Jewish Galilean: A New Reading of the Jesus Story*, London: T & T Clarke, 2004: 24–59, at 59. See also Edward Echlin, *Earth Spirituality: Jesus at the Centre*, New Alresford: Arthur James, 199.

31 Richard Bauckham, 'Reading the Synoptic Gospels Ecologically', in *Ecological Hermeneutics: Biblical, Historical and Theological Perspectives*, edited by David G. Horrell, Cherryl Hunt, Christopher Southgate and Francesca Stavrakopoulou, London: T & T Clarke, 2010: 70–82, at 73. A similar observation on the teaching of Jesus and the natural world can be found in Michael Drumm, with specific reference to the Gospel of Matthew. See Michael Drumm, 'Being Educated in Communion', in *Proceedings of the International Symposium of Theology: The Ecclesiology of Communion 50 Years after Vatican II*, Dublin: Veritas Publications, 2013: 238–49, at 239.

32 Elizabeth A. Johnson, *Ask the Beasts*, op. cit., 268.

33 *Summa Theologiae*, 1. 8. 1, as quoted by Elizabeth A. Johnson, in *Ask the Beasts*, op. cit., 146, n.33.

34 Ibid., 1. 47. 1.

35 Denis Edwards, *Ecology at the Heart of Faith*, New York, NY: Orbis Books, 2006: 78.

36 Where does this leave Jesus? Terrence Tilley addresses this question in a slightly different context. His answer, however, is relevant to the question just posed. He replies that historically Jesus can be understood truly as 'first among equals', and that theologically this same Jesus came to be the one worshipped as truly God's agent. See Terrence Tilley, *The Disciples' Jesus: Christology as Reconciling Practice*, New York, NY: Orbis Books: 2008: 41–49, at 49.

37 Leslie Muray, 'Human Uniqueness vs. Human Distinctiveness: The *Imago Dei* in the Kinship of all Creatures', in *American Journal of Theology and Philosophy*, 2007: 306.

38 A further discussion of these issues can be found in Elizabeth A. Johnson, *Ask the Beasts*, op. cit.,143–50; Denis Edwards, *Ecology at the Heart of Faith*, op. cit., 74–78, and Daniel Horan, *All God's Creatures*, op. cit., 124–137; Leslie Muray, art. cit.

39 This question is addressed in greater depth and detail by a helpful and stimulating article by Carmody T. S. Grey entitled '"The only creature God willed for its own sake": Anthropocentrism in *Laudato Si'* and *Gaudium et Spes'*, in *Modern Theology*, 2019, DOI:10.111/ moth12588.1–19. This article came to my attention after the completion of this chapter.

Endnotes Chapter 7

1 Caroline Merchant, *Women, Ecology and the Scientific Revolution*, New York, NY: Harper and Row, 1980.

2 This term is used to good effect by Roger Haight in 'Spirituality, Evolution, Creator God', in *Theological Studies*, 2018, Vol. 79 (2), 251–73.

3 Augustine, *The City of God*, Book 16, and *Sermons*, 68.6.

4 Simon Oliver, *Creation: A Guide for the Perplexed*, London: Bloomsbury T & T Clark, 2017, 101.

5 Thomas Berry, *The Great Work: Our Way into the Future*, New York, NY: Random House, 1999: 82.

6   Denis Edwards, '"Sublime Communion": The Theology of the Natural World in *Laudato Si*', in *Theological Studies*, June 2016: 377–91, at 380 and 383.

7   Mircea Eliade, *The Sacred and the Profane: The Nature of Religion*, New York, NY: Harcourt, Brace & World, 1959: 179, as quoted in Anthony J. Kelly, *Laudato Si': An Integral Ecology and the Catholic Vision*, Australia: ATF Press Publishing Group, 2016: 111.

8   This creation-centred view of the Eucharist is also found in the work of John Zizioulas (1931–), currently serving as Ecumenical Patriarch of the Orthodox Church, and also in some of the writings of the early Fathers of the Church. For reasons of space, we must confine ourselves to Francis's papal predecessors and Teilhard de Chardin SJ.

9   This 'Mass on the World' is available in Pierre Teilhard de Chardin SJ, *Hymn of the Universe*, London: Collins, 1965: 13–37.

10   St John Paul II, *Gift and Mystery*, New York: Image, 1996: 73.

11   St John Paul II, *Ecclesia de Eucharistia: On the Eucharist in its relation to the Church*, April 2003: a.8.

12   Benedict XVI, *Homily for the Mass of Corpus Domini*, 15 June 2006. The word 'host' has many meanings in English. Is it possible to think of the cosmos/earth as being host to humanity?

13   Aosta, 24 July 2009. In this quotation, Benedict is picking up on something that the theologian Joseph Cardinal Ratzinger had written in 2000: 'Against the background of the modern evolutionary world-view, Teilhard depicted the *cosmos* as a process of assent … From here, Teilhard went on to give new meaning to Christian worship: The transubstantiated host is the anticipation of the transformation and divinisation of matter in Christological fullness. In his view, the Eucharist provides the movement of the *cosmos* with its direction, it anticipates its goal and, at the same time, urges it on', Joseph Ratzinger, *The Spirit of the Liturgy*, San Francisco, CA: Ignatius Press, 2000: 29.

14   'The Mass on the World', in *Hymn of the Universe*, op. cit., 19.

15   Ibid., 19–37.

16   See Catherine Vince, *Worship and the New Cosmology: Liturgical and Theological Challenges*, Collegeville, MN: Liturgical Press, 2014: 16–19.

17   On this theme of cosmology and liturgy, see some preliminary remarks in Dermot Lane, 'Praying the New Cosmology', in *The Furrow*, September 2018: 474–79.

18   Teilhard de Chardin SJ, *Science and Christ*, London: Collins, 1968: 64–66.

19   John C. Haughey, 'Teilhard de Chardin: The Empirical Mystic', in *From Teilhard to Omega: Co-creating an Unfinished Universe*, edited by Ilia Delio, New York, NY: Orbis Books, 2014: 210.

20   William R. Stoeger, 'Scientific accounts of ultimate catastrophes in our life-bearing Universe', *The end of the world and the ends of God*, edited by John Polkinghorne and Michael Welker, Harrisburg, PA: Trinity Press International, 2000:19–28, at 28.

21   Margaret Daly Denton, *John: An Earth Bible Commentary. Supposing him to be the Gardener*, London: Bloomsbury, 2017: 162. In examining the background to John 12:24, Daly discerns a link with the Wisdom traditions of Israel.

22   John F. Haught, *The New Cosmic Story: Inside Our Awakening Universe*, New Haven, CT: Yale University Press, 2017: 45; see also 17 and 9.

23   Robert Daly, 'Ecological Euchology', in *Worship*, March 2015: 167.

24   Part of the draft Eucharistic prayer is available in his article in *Worship*, March 2015.

25   Thomas Reese, 'Eucharistic Prayer in the 21st Century', in *National Catholic Reporter*, 12 January 2017.

26   Joris Geldhof, 'Fruit of the Earth, Work of Human Hands, Bread of Life: The *Ordo Missae* on Creation and the World', in *Full of Your Glory: Liturgy, Cosmos, Creation*, edited by Teresa Berger, Collegeville, MN: Liturgical Press, 2019: 245–65.

27   Ibid., 257.

28   Ibid.

29   Ibid., 255.

30   *The Constitution on the Sacred Liturgy*, 1963, a. 14.

31   This quotation from Holmes Rolston III is taken from Mikael Stenmark, *How to Relate Science and Religion: A Multidimensional model*, Grand Rapids, MI: Wm. B. Eerdmans, 2004: 266.

32   Aurora Leigh, *Poetical Works of Elizabeth Barrett Browning*, New York: 1897: 466.

Select Bibliography

OF BOOKS on theology and ecology, there is no end! The following is a select sample.

Barker, Margaret, *Creation: A Biblical Vision for the Environment*, London: T&T Clark International, 2010.

Bauckham, Richard, *The Bible and Ecology: Rediscovering the Community of Creation*, London: Darton, Longman & Todd, 2010.

Bergant, Dianne, *A New Heaven, A New Earth: The Bible and Catholicity*, New York, NY: Orbis Books, 2016.

Berger, Theresa (ed.), *Full of your Glory: Liturgy, Cosmos, Creation*, Collegeville, MN: Liturgical Press, 2019.

Brown, William P., *The Seven Pillars of Creation: The Bible, Science and the Ecology of Wonder*, Oxford: Oxford University Press, 2010.

Carrol, Denis, *Towards a Story of the Earth: Essays in the theology of Creation*, Dublin: Dominican Publications, 1987

Castelo, Daniel, *Pneumatology: A Guide for the Perplexed*, New York, NY: Bloomsbury T&T Clark, 2015.

Conradie, Ernst M., Bergmann, Sigurd, Deane-Drummond Celia, and Edwards, Denis (eds.), *Christian Faith and the Earth: Current Paths and Emerging Horizons in Eco-Theology*, New York, NY: Bloomsbury T&T Clark, 2014.

Cronin, Michael, *Eco-Translation: Translation and Ecology in the Age of Anthropocene*, London: Routledge, 2017.

Daly Denton, Margaret, *John: An Earth Bible Commentary: Supposing Him to Be the Gardener*, London: Bloomsbury T&T Clark, 2017.

Daly, Gabriel, *Creation and Redemption*, Dublin: Gill and Macmillan, 1988.

Delio, Ilia (ed.), *From Teilhard to Omega: Co-creating an Unfinished Universe*, New York, NY: Orbis Books, 2014.

— *Making All Things New: Catholicity, Cosmology, Consciousness*, New York, NY: Orbis Books, 2015.

DiLeo, Dan (ed.), *All Creation is Connected: Voices in Response to Pope Francis's Encyclical on Ecology*, Winona, MN: Anselm Academic, 2018.

Edwards, Denis (ed.), *Earth Revealing – Earth Healing: Ecology and Christian Theology*, Collegeville, MN: Liturgical Press, 2001.

— *Ecology at the Heart of Faith: The Change of Heart that Leads to a New Way of Living on Earth*, New York, NY: Orbis Books, 2006.

— *How God Acts: Creation, Redemption, and Special Divine Action*, Minneapolis, MN: Fortress Press, 2010.

— *Christian Understandings of Creation: The Historical Trajectory*, Minneapolis, MN: Fortress Press, 2017.

— *The Natural World and God: Theological Explorations*, Adelaide, ATF Press, 2017.

— *Deep Incarnation: God's Redemptive Suffering with Creatures*, New York, NY: Orbis Books, 2019.

Fretheim, Terence E., *God on the World in the Old Testament: A Relational Theology of Creation*, Nashville, TN: Abington Press, 2005.

Gold, Lorna, *Climate Generation: Awakening to our Children's Future*, Dublin: Veritas Publications, 2018.

Gregersen, Niels Henrik (ed.), *Incarnation: On the Scope and Depth of Christology*, Philadelphia, PA: Fortress Press, 2013.

Haught, John F., *The Promise of Nature: Ecology and Cosmic Purpose*, Mahwah, NJ: Paulist Press, 1993.

— *Resting on the Future: Catholic Theology for an Unfinished Universe*, New York, NY: Bloomsbury, 2015.

— *The New Cosmic Story: Inside our Awakening Universe*, New Haven, CT: Yale University Press, 2017.

Horan, Daniel P., *All God's Creatures: A Theology of Creation*, New York, NY: Lexington Books/Fortress Academic, 2018.

Irwin, Kevin W., *A Commentary on Laudato Si': Examining the Background, Contributions, Implementation, and Future of Pope Francis's Encyclical*, Mahwah, NJ: Paulist Press, 2016.

Johnson, Elizabeth A., *Women, Earth, and Creator Spirit*, The 1993 Madeleva Lecture in Spirituality, Mahwah, NJ: Paulist Press, 1993.

— *Ask the Beasts: Darwin and the God of Love*, New York, NY: Bloomsbury Continuum, 2014.

— *Abounding in Kindness: Writings for the People of God*, New York: Orbis Books, 2015.

— *Creation and the Cross: The Mercy of God for a Planet in Peril*, New York, NY: Orbis Books, 2018.

Kelly, Anthony J., *Laudato Si': An Integral Ecology and the Catholic Vision*, Adelaide: ATF Press, 2016.

— *Integral Ecology and the Fullness of Life: Theological and Philosophical Perspectives*, Mahwah, NJ: Paulist Press, 2018.

Klein, Naomi, *On Fire: The Burning Case for a Green New Deal*, London: Allen Lane, an imprint of Penguin books, 2019.

Lennan, Richard, and Pineda-Madrid Nancy (eds.), *Hope: Promise, Possibility and Fulfilment*, Mahwah, NJ: Paulist Press, 2013.

— *The Holy Spirit: Setting the World on Fire,* Mahwah, NJ: Paulist Press, 2017.

McDonagh, Sean, *To Care for the Earth: A Call to a New Theology,* London: Chapman, 1986.

— *On care for our Common Home, Laudato Si': the Encyclical of Pope Francis on the environment, with comments by Seán McDonagh*, New York, NY: Orbis Books, 2016.

— (ed.) *Laudato Si', An Irish Response: Essays on the Pope's letter on the Environment*, Dublin: Veritas Publications, 2017.

McKim, Robert, *Laudato Si' and the Environment: Pope Francis's Green Encyclical*, London: Routledge, 2020.

Mickey, Sam, Kelly, Sean, and Robert, Adam (eds.), *The Variety of Integral Ecologies: Nature, Culture, and Knowledge in the Planetary Era*, New York, NY: SUNY Press, 2017.

Miller, Vincent J. (ed.), *The Theological and Ecological Vision of Laudato Si': Everything is Connected*, New York, NY: Bloomsbury T&T Clark, 2017.

Northcott, Michael S., and Scott, Peter M. (eds.), *Systematic Theology and Climate Change:*

Ecumenical Perspectives, London: Routledge, 2014.

Oliver, Simon, *Creation: A Guide for the Perplexed*, London: Bloomsbury, 2017.

Robinson, Mary, *Climate Justice: Hope, Resilience and the Fight for a Sustainable Future*, London: Bloomsbury, 2018.

Russell, Robert J., *Cosmology, Evolution and Resurrection Hope: Theology and Science in Creative Mutual Interaction*, Ontario: Pandora Press, 2006.

Scheid, Daniel P., *The Cosmic Common Good: Religious Grounds for Ecological Ethics*, New York, NY: Oxford University Press, 2016

Teilhard de Chardin, Pierre, *Hymn of the Universe*, London: Collins, 1965.

Thiselton, Anthony C., *The Holy Spirit: in Biblical Teaching Through the Centuries, and Today*, Grand Rapids, MI: William B. Eerdmans, 2013.

Thunberg, Greta, *No One is Too Small to Make a Difference*, London: Penguin Books, 2019.

Tilley, Terrence, W., *The Disciples' Jesus: Christology as Reconciling Practice*, New York, NY: Orbis Books, 2008.

Tucker, Mary Evelyn (ed.). *Thomas Berry, The Sacred Universe: Earth, Spirituality and Religion in the 21st Century*, with a Foreword by Mary Evelyn Tucker, New York, NY: Columbia University Press, 2009.

Tucker, Mary Evelyn, and Grimm John (eds.), *Living Cosmology: Christian Responses to Journey of the Universe*, New York, NY: Orbis Books, 2016.

Tucker, Mary Evelyn, Grimm, John, and Angyal, Andrew, *Thomas Berry: A Biography*, New York, NY: Columbia University Press, 2019.

Uhl, Christopher , *Developing Ecological Consciousness: The End of Separation*, 2nd edition, New York, NY: Rowman and Littlefield Publishers, 2013.

Vince, Catherine, *Worship and the New Cosmology: Liturgical and Theological Challenges,* Collegeville, MN: Liturgical Press, 2014.

Quotations from the Second Vatican Council documents are taken from Vatican Council II: Constitutions, Decrees, Declarations, ed. by Austin Flannery OP, a completely revised translation in inclusive language, Dublin: Dominican publications, 1996

Biblical quotations are taken from the New Revised Standard Version Bible, New York: Oxford University Press, 1991, unless otherwise stated

Index